Fundamentals of Investments
in U.S.
Financial Markets

Fundamentals of Investments in U.S. Financial Markets

A comprehensive educational resource
book for gaining knowledge and understanding
of investments in U.S. financial markets.

Jack D. Howell, Jr.

Published by: The American Institute
For Financial Education

a publication of

The American Institute
For Financial Education

Financial Resource Publishers

Published in the United States of America by:

The American Institute
For Financial Education
4920 Roswell Road, Suite 45B-508
Atlanta, GA 30342

Library of Congress Catalog Card Number: 98-72410

Howell, Jack D., Jr.
    Fundamentals of Investments in U.S. Financial Markets
1. Investments. 2. Stocks. 3. Bonds. 4. Mutual Funds.
5. Retirement Plans. 6. Securities Analysis.

ISBN 978-0-9668050-4-8
ISBN   0-9668050-4-6

"This publication is designed to provide accurate and authoritative information in regard to the subject matter covered. It is sold with the understanding that the publisher is not engaged in rendering legal, accounting, or other professional service. If legal advice or expert assistance is required, the services of a competent professional person should be sought."
–From a Declaration of Principles jointly adopted by a Committee of the American Bar Association and a Committee of the Publishers and Associations.

Artwork by: Romerofisk . . . Marketing Designs Solutions, Inc., Dayton, Ohio

Printed in the United States of America   2nd Edition

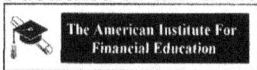

Dedication

> To the individual investor,
> who has sought a comprehensive
> investment education resource book
> detailing the intricacies of the financial
> markets.

Acknowledgments

I must, first and foremost, recognize and acknowledge my family and friends who have contributed with inspiration, encouragement, and unwavering support. They willingly gave their time and assistance in many ways, none more helpful than their participation in discussions of the subject matter for clarity.

Also, I would like to recognize those who gave very generously of their time in reviewing, critiquing, and offering constructive suggestions.

I am very grateful to "Romerofisk . . . Marketing Design Solutions, Inc." for their invaluable assistance with the graphic arts design and production.

Also, my thanks goes to all the clients over the last 17 years who have asked me to recommend a book of this nature. They, unknowingly, provided the impetus for me to begin and complete this book.

Lastly, but certainly not least, I must acknowledge and give thanks to the giver and sustainer of all life, ... the Almightly, for mine.

Table of Contents

Preface

I think it is important to state the goals and objectives of this book, and what the reader should and should not expect to gain from reading it.

First, let's review the goals and objectives. Through my experience in the financial markets, over 20 years as an investor and nearly 10 years as a licensed stockbroker, I have had the thoroughly enjoyable experience of interacting with literally thousands of individual investors and aspiring investors. Particularly, over the last 5 years, as the stock market has reached higher and higher record levels, there has been an abundance of new investors entering the financial marketplace. On many occasions these individuals have requested the referral of any book or any resource which would provide a basic overview of the financial markets, and show them how to transact business in the financial markets. As much as I would have liked to suggest a literary resource, there was no comprehensive text available. There were many books on the market, but they were mostly written for the more experienced and sophisticated investor, and were generally focused on one specific topic. There was an incredible void of comprehensive literary resources written specifically for the beginning and intermediate level investor. As the years passed, and the requests for this type of resource continued to increase, I decided to tackle this void and write a concise, comprehensive, and "reader friendly" resource for the average individual investor. While the objective of this book is to educate the novice and intermediate level investor to the intricacies of the financial markets, I have met very few investors, during my ten year tenure as a stockbroker, who would not benefit from the information in this book. I believe this book will add to the knowledge base, irrespective of experience level, of all who read this financial resource.

Second, let's go over what this book will and will not accomplish for the reader. This book will NOT take the inexperienced or experienced investor and transform them into "master trader". This book will NOT teach the reader how to make a "million" dollars over the next 12 months. Lastly, this book will NOT provide all the information investors will ever need to know about the financial markets, for the markets are dynamic and diverse. Continuing education is always required for the astute investor.

This book WILL, however, educate individual investors to the basic terminology and structure of the financial markets. This book WILL teach the reader the basics of how to invest, how to conduct basic financial and technical analysis, and it WILL educate the investor to the potential risks that are present in the financial markets. This book WILL through an in-depth review, give the reader the knowledge necessary to feel comfortable and confident when investing in stocks, bonds, or mutual funds. Lastly, while this book is not the "end all" of financial marketplace education, it WILL provide a diverse and comprehensive study of the financial markets, while also serving as a valuable long-term resource book for the investor's personal library.

1

Equity Securities

"...The greater thing in this world,
is not so much where we stand
as in what direction we are going..."

Oliver Wendell Holmes
(1809-94)
American physician and author

Equity Securities

I believe it is appropriate to begin the discussion of stock's with asking the very basic question; What is a stock? Stocks are a form of ownership in a corporation. Corporate ownership is represented by an "equity" position, therefore stocks are commonly referred to as equity securities.

There are two broad classes of stock: **Common and Preferred**.

Common Stock

Authorized Stock

When a corporation is formed, its corporate charter will state a fixed number of common shares which may be issued. This stated amount of stock, authorized by the corporations board of directors is termed "authorized stock". This stock is usually assigned an arbitrarily low value such as 1 cent or 1 dollar per share. This arbitrary value is called "**par value**". The par value has no bearing on the market value of the stock. The par value is generally only used for taxable reasons. For example, a state may impose a tax on the corporation based upon the par value of the corporations shares, therefore corporations usually set the par value of shares as low as possible.

Issued Stock

Usually, the corporation issuing stock does not issue its entire authorized allocation, because to do so would require the corporation to seek an amended charter from the Board of Directors. Therefore, the corporation will generally **issue** only a portion of its authorized shares. For example, if a corporation has the authority to issue 5 million shares, as stated in its charter, it might only issue 1 million shares and reserve the right to issue the remaining shares at a later date. In the above example, the corporation has 1 million shares issued in the marketplace.

Outstanding Shares

The shares actually in the marketplace are termed "**outstanding**" shares. Will the amount of issued shares equal the amount outstanding? No. Why?

Because the corporation might decide to buy back some of its shares in the open market. If it does, these shares are referred to as **treasury** shares. Treasury shares do not have voting rights nor do they receive any dividends. Also, earning per share is based only on the number of shares outstanding. Treasury stock is not considered to be **outstanding** stock.

Treasury Stock

As just stated, when a corporation acquires its own stock it is referred to as treasury stock. Treasury stock does not vote, receive dividends, nor effect the equity of existing shareholders. It may be resold, used for various incentive plans, or used to acquire additional assets at any time in the future.

Public Offering Price

When a corporation decides to sell stock to the public for the first time, the stock offering is referred to as a **new issue**. A new issue is sold at a **public offering price**.This price is determined by several factors including but not limited to:
      1) sales and earnings of corporation;
      2) estimated future growth;
      3) demand for shares;
      4) industry evaluation and comparisons;
      5) overall market conditions

All of these factors, and others, play a role in determining what is commonly referred to as the **Initial Public Offering** or **IPO** price. Once the IPO shares have been sold, the stock will begin trading in the secondary market at a price that is called the current market price. This price is determined by the natural laws of demand and supply and may or may not have any relevance to the IPO price.

Par Value As stated earlier, a company's stock may be assigned a par value. This value has no relationship to its market value and is in fact, sometime set at zero. A stocks par value is only relevant to certain corporate taxation strategies.

Common Shareholder Rights

Right to Inspect Books & Records Common shareholders have a right to inspect the books and records of the company. In practice, however, this doesn't happen very often because audited financial statements are required by the Securities and Exchange Commission to be sent to shareholders on an annual basis.

Right to Transfer Ownership Common shareholders have the right to sell their shares to anyone else without restriction. Common stocks are negotiable securities and can be traded. Certain securities are non-negotiable and cannot be traded.

Right to Corp. Distributions If the Board of Directors decides to pay a cash dividend, stock dividend, or split its stock, the common shareholder has the right to his or her pro rata share of these distributions. Most corporations pay cash dividends quarterly.

Right to Corp. Assets Upon Dissolution If the corporation goes bankrupt, the common shareholders have the right to the assets of the corporation **after** all other claimholders have been paid. That's right, the common shareholder is paid **last**.

Preemptive Right If a corporation decides to issue additional shares, common shareholders have a "preemptive" right to maintain proportionate ownership in the company. Common shareholders have the right to purchase the shares before anyone else. The offer of these shares to existing shareholders is called a "**Rights Offering**."

Common shareholders have the right to vote at the annual meeting. They vote on the Board of Directors and on matters that affect the shareholders "**ownership interest**." Each shareholder receives 1 vote per share. Therefore, an investor with 100 shares will receive 100 votes on each item being voted on that year. There are two types of voting; **statutory** and **cumulative**. Assume 3 directorships are open, with statutory voting, 100 votes maximum are allowed per director. Under cumulative voting rules, 3 directorships x 100 votes = 300 total votes. The shareholder could vote 100 shares for each directorship, or cast all 300 votes for just 1 directorship. When a shareholder is unable to attend the annual meeting, a card called a "**proxy**" is filled out and mailed to the company. At the annual meeting the **proxy** vote will be tallied according to its owners instructions.

Proxy

Shareholder Recordkeeping

Owners Name The shares of a corporation must be registered somewhere in order for the corporation to have an accurate accounting for the name and address of all shareholders. Common shareholders currently have a choice of whether to have the shares registered in the owners name and to receive the physical certificates, or to have the shares registered in book entry form.

Street Name Book entry is commonly referred to in the industry as "**Street Name**." When a stock is registered in street name, there is no physical certificate issued, nor is the owners name registered with the issuing corporations transfer agent. Rather, the ownership is registered with the clearing corporation, usually the brokerage firm, which settles the trades.

Transfer Agent

The corporation hires an outside firm, usually a bank or trust company, to act as **transfer agent**. Every day, as trades of the stock settle, a report is made to the transfer agent. The transfer agent then cancels the "**sold**" shares and issues new shares in the name of the **buyer**. The transfer agent keeps an accurate record of the shareholders updated daily. The transfer agent also usually handles the duties of mailing corporate information to shareholders (e.g. dividend information, corporate reports, and voting material).

Registrar

The corporation also hires an outside firm, usually a bank or trust Registrar company, to serve in the capacity of **registrar**. The registrar also maintains a record of all shareholder names and addresses and is given the responsibility of ensuring that the company does not issue more shares than authorized under the company's charter. The registrar acts as a watchdog over the transfer agent. Transfer agents can, and have, made mistakes, such as canceling 100 shares and transferring those shares to the new owner as 1000 shares. The registrar is supposed to catch these mistakes and correct them.

Dividends

A) Cash Dividends

Declaration Date

When a corporation decides to pay a cash dividend, the corporation announces this decision by making what is called **dividend declaration**. When this declaration is made, there are three distinctive dates which usually accompany it.

Ex-Dividend Date

First is the **ex-dividend date**. The prefix "**ex**" means **without**. Therefore, the ex-dividend date is the first date that the stock trades without the dividend. Following, if the investor wishes to receive the dividend for the current quarter, he or she must purchase the stock **prior to** the ex-dividend date.

Record Date

The second date is the **record date**. The record date is the date that the company's transfer agent will consult the records of the company and will pay the dividend to every stockholder of record as of the close of business on that date.

Payable Date

The third relevant date is the **payable date**. This is the date, as you might have already guessed, that the dividend will be mailed or paid to the stockholder. If the investor holds the physical stock certificate, the dividend will be mailed from the transfer agent directly to the shareholder. However, if the investor has shares held in "**street name**", the transfer agent has no record of these individual shareholders, therefore the dividend is credited in sum total to the clearing corporation and the clearing corporation disburses the dividend to the individual accounts of the shareholders.

The sample calendar below depicts these dates:

JULY 200X

Declaration Date	S	M	T	W	T	F	S
				1	2	3	4	Record Date
	5	6	7	8	9	10	11
	12	13	14	15	16	17	18
Ex-Dividend Date	19	20	21	22	23	24	25
	26	27	28	29	30	31	Payable Date

Given the above dates, the investor would have to purchase the stock no later than **Monday 13**, to be entitled to the dividend payment.

One final note on cash dividends. On the ex-dividend date, the stock price will be reduced by the amount of the cash dividend. For example, lets say we have a stock trading currently at $10.00, and the company has announced a dividend of 50 cents. Also, assume the stock closes the day before the ex-dividend date at $10.00 per share. The following day, the ex-dividend date, the stock will reflect a closing price of $9.50 instead of $10.00 due to the reduction of the dividend amount.

B) Stock Dividends
& Splits

A company may decide to pay a stock dividend instead of or in combination with a cash dividend. Stock dividends come in many different sizes; determined by the company's Board of Directors. They have the same 3 relevant dates as cash dividends. Those are ex-dividend dates, record dates, and payable dates.

There is, however, one important distinction to make with respect to stock splits. The ex-dividend date is the first date in a cash dividend, but it is the last date in a stock split. In a stock split, the ex-dividend date is the first business day after the payable date. Why? Well remember, that the ex-dividend date is the first day the stock trades without the dividend. Therefore, since an investor may purchase a stock up to and including the payable date and receive the stock split, then by definition the ex-dividend date has to be after the payable date.

Other Equity Securities

Rights
We have already covered the shareholders "preemptive right" to maintain proportionate ownership in the com-

pany. If a company wants to issue new shares, it must give existing shareholder the first opportunity to purchase the new shares. This is called a "**Rights Offering**." In a rights offering, existing shareholders are able to buy these shares below the current market price. This discount reflects the amount that would have to be paid to an underwriter if the issue were sold to the public. To handle the mechanics of the offering, the company hires a "**rights agent**." This is usually the existing transfer agent of the corporation. If all of the shares are not subscribed to by existing shareholders, the issuer will usually have an underwriter on "standby" to pick up the remaining shares. The underwriter then resells these shares to the public. Since existing shareholders have the right to buy the stock for less than the market price, their subscription rights have value. Shareholders are free to exercise their rights or sell them in the open market, however they must act quickly because rights offerings generally expire in 30 to 60 days.

Warrants

Warrant Attached To New Stock Or Bond Issue

A warrant is a long term option to buy stock at a fixed price. Warrants are usually attached to the sale of a new stock or bond issue as a "sweetener" to make the issue more attractive.

Long Term Option To Buy Stock

For Example, a new issue is being sold as a "**unit**" consisting of 1 common share and 1 warrant to purchase an additional common share. The common stock is valued at $20 and the warrant allows the holder to purchase an additional share at $30. The warrant expires in five years.

Warrants usually have a "wait" period before they can be

exercised (e.g. 1 year). After the wait period it can be exercised at the set price until expiration. Of course, it makes no sense to exercise unless the market price of the stock is equal to or above the exercise price of the warrant.

Thus, warrants have an indeterminate value at issuance. But they are worth something and therefore allow the issuer to raise the price of the issue to which the warrant is attached.

Warrants are almost always issued at a substantial premium to the stock's current market or IPO price and only gain additional value if the common stock price rises. For example, assume that this warrant is valued in the market at $1. If the market price of the stock moves to $35 warrant will be worth at least $5 since it allows the purchase of the stock at $30 per share. Other factors such as the general outlook for the company and the time duration remaining until expiration may also effect the price of the warrants.

Perpetual Warrants

Warrants usually have a life span of 5 years, however, the company may issue warrants for any amount of time and may even issue "perpetual warrants". They trade separately from the common stock on the exchange where the stock is listed.

Difference Between Rights and Warrants

Do not confuse a **right** with a **warrant**. A **warrant** is usually a "long term" investment, with the purchase of shares at a later date at a fixed exercise price prior to the warrants expiration date. **Rights**, conversely, are "short term". The corporation needs to raise the additional funds now, and if its existing stockholders will not exercise, the corporation will turn to the general public.

Proportional Ownership A critical difference is that warrants have no relationship with proportionate ownership of the corporation. Unlike rights which are sent to existing stockholders, warrants must be purchased in the open market or are sometimes found attached to other securities. Also, while the issuer determines the number of rights necessary to purchase each additional share of new stock, the terms of a warrant almost always give the holder the right to purchase one share for each warrant held. Warrants are frequently referred to as a call option with a very long expiration.

Warrants as Sweetners As mentioned earlier, warrants are sometimes attached to other securities, frequently debt securities. These warrants are generally referred to as "**sweeteners**." Since a warrant gives the holder the right to buy the stock at a predetermined price, if the common stock should go up, the warrant could become quite valuable. Attaching warrants to debt securities, at no additional charge to buyers, can make the debt securities more attractive to investors. Anything that will make the bond more attractive, make the investment a little "sweeter", will usually result in the issuer being able to borrow at a lower interest rate, and this, of course, is beneficial to the issuing corporation. Warrants are often used as bond "sweeteners."

AMERICAN DEPOSITORY RECEIPTS (ADRs)

ADRs Are A Vehicle for Trading Foreign Securities in The U.S. Foreign companies can "list" their shares for trading on stock exchanges in the U. S. For example, investors can buy shares of Sony or Volvo (both foreign companies) on US stock exchanges. When these "shares" are bought, instead of receiving actual stock, the buyer receives certificates that represent the actual shares. These certificates are called **American Depository Receipts**.

Many foreign companies do not want their actual shares traded in the U.S. because the shares have to be registered in the U.S. with the Securities and Exchange Commission, and the company must follow SEC reporting rules. Adhering to these rules is time consuming and expensive.

Bank Holds Foreign Securities In Country of Origin

These companies let someone else bother with all of these requirements–usually a large international bank with offices in the country where company is headquartered. The bank will buy up blocks of the stock and place it in trust in the country of origin. Depository Receipts are backed by the securities held in trust. The ADRs are registered with the SEC and sold in the U.S. As dividend payments are received, the bank passes these on to the receipt holder. But the receipt holder does

No Voting or Preemptive Rights

not have voting or preemptive rights. The bank votes the shares that it owns and it will sell off preemptive rights and remit the money to the receipt holder.

Sponsored ADRs

An ADR can represent one share of the underlying stock, or multiple shares. All exchange listed ADRs are "**sponsored**," that is, the foreign company "sponsors" the issue to increase its worldwide ownership base. Sponsored ADRs only use one depository bank which is appointed by the issuer. Issuers that sponsor ADRs provide quarterly and annual financial reports to shareholders in English. Sponsored ADRs are often called American Depository Shares or ADSs.

Non-Sponsored ADRs

Non-Sponsored ADRs are assembled by banks and broker-dealers without the issuer's participation. An unsponsored program may have more than one depository bank, since the issuer does not participate in any way. Holders of non-sponsored ADRs only receive annual financial reports in the language of the issuer. Non-sponsored ADRs trade in the "over-the-counter" market.

The New York Stock Exchange has been aggressively pursuing large foreign companies to list their ADRs on the NYSE. As of this writing, there are approximately 1100 ADRs traded in the United States on all of the exchanges and in the "over-the-counter" market.

Dividend Declared in Foreign Currency

As a final note on the subject, dividends on ADRs are declared by the foreign company in the local currency, and are then converted into U.S. dollars and remitted to the receipt holders by the intermediary bank. The market prices of ADRs will therefore be influenced not only by the performance of the company's stock, but also by foreign currency exchange fluctuations.

Foreign Taxes

With respect to dividends received from ADRs, the country of origin can withhold local taxes, but such taxes can be claimed as a credit against U.S. taxes due on dividends received.

PREFERRED STOCK

Equity Security

Preferred Claim to Assets

Like common stock, preferred stock is also an equity security, that is, it represents shares of ownership in the corporation that issues it. Perhaps, the best way to explain the characteristics of preferred stock, is to outline the differences between **preferred** and **common** stock. First, why is the term "**preferred**" used. A preferred stockholder has preference in claims to dividends and assets ahead of the common stockholder should there be a bankruptcy liquidation. Preferred shareholders get paid first! However, please note, this preference only relates to common stockholders. Because preferred stock is an equity security, it has no claims on assets until all creditors have been satisfied.

Fixed Rate Dividend

A second difference: while dividends on **common** stock may fluctuate from year to year based upon the corporations earnings and the desires of management, **preferred** stock dividends are paid at a **fixed rate**.

Par Value

Another major difference is that **par value** while not important to common stockholders, **is important** to preferred stockholders because it is usually this figure upon which the dividend is calculated. The dividend is usually stated as a percentage of par value. For example, if a preferred stock has a par value of $100 and the stated dividend rate is 8%, the investor, will receive $8 per year for each share of this particular preferred stock. If the preferred stock does not have a par value, then the dividend will be stated as a fixed number of dollars per year. In the above example, if this preferred had no par value, it would be called an $8 preferred, referring to its $8 annual dividend.

No Voting or Preemptive Rights

One last difference between preferred and common stock is that preferred stockholders usually do not have voting or preemptive rights.

There are some special features frequently found with preferred stocks. Not **all preferred** stocks carry these features. Some preferred have all, others have none, and others may have a combination.

Cumulative

The first feature is a **cumulative dividend provision**. If a company is unable to pay its preferred dividend, the cumulative dividend provision provides that the corporation must pay all dividends in arrears and current dividends owed, before it can pay any dividends to common shareholders. Of course, there is no guarantee that the corporation will ever be able to pay the dividend. If the company were to liquidate, the arrearage would be a prior claim ahead of common's residual interest.

If a preferred stock is **non-cumulative**, it means that if a corporation skips a dividend payment, the investor receives nothing for that quarter and has no further claim upon the corporation's earnings. However, just as with the cumulative, if the corporation skips the non-cumulative preferred dividend for that quarter, it cannot pay any dividend on the common for that quarter either.

The terms cumulative and non-cumulative merely refer to accumulating unpaid dividends from prior periods or not doing so, respectively.

Convertible   One of the most attractive features a preferred stock can have is a provision for conversion. Convertible preferred stock can be exchanged for a fixed number of common shares of the issuing company at the investor's discretion. If the common stock moves up sharply, convertible preferred, because it can be exchanged for the common, tends to move up as well. Therefore, this conversion feature provides the investor with growth potential in addition to the fixed income which is standard with any preferred stock.

Callable   Another feature is **Callability**. This is a feature that permits the corporation to redeem (buy back) its preferred stock at a fixed price from the investors at some time in the future. While it is true that the corporation could buy back its preferred stock in the marketplace, there would be an uncertainty, to the issuer, as to what the total cost of the buyback would be since market prices are set by supply and demand. The corporation, by its action, is increasing demand and reducing supply. At the time of issuance, the call price (the price the issuing corporation may elect to pay for the shares) is stated on the stock certificate. Does the corporation have to call in its preferred shares? Of course not. The corporation will only call in the shares if interest rates have fallen. Once the old preferred shares have been retired, the corporation usually will issue new preferred shares at the current lower interest rates.

Participating

Participating preferred stock is unique (there are only a handful of them left) in that it is the only preferred stock that, in addition to a stated fixed dividend, is also eligible to **participate** in the common stocks dividend or some other "special" common stock dividend. A typical participating preferred might give, in addition to a stated fixed dividend, shareholders 50% (or 75%, or 100%) of the per share dividend received by common stockholders. The special dividend might apply as follows. After having an exceptionally strong year, the Board of Directors declares a "**special**" year-end dividend of $5.00. The preferred as well as the common will receive this dividend if the preferred has a "**participating**" feature.

Performance Preferred

Sometimes, participating preferred stock is referred to "performance preferred," because the preferred shareholders are able to receive a higher dividend amount if the company's performance is better than usual.

Adjustable Rate

Adjustable Rate Preferred: This is a relatively new type of preferred stock. Instead of paying a "**fixed**" dividend rate, the dividend rate is "reset" periodically (usually once a year) to an index of market rates. If interest rates rise, the rate will increase at the reset date. Conversely, if interest rates fall, the rate will decrease at the reset date. Sometimes this type of issue is called a "reset" preferred.

Preference Ranking The last feature we will discuss is the ranking of **preference** and degree of preference upon dissolution. Frequently, a corporation has more than one class of preferred stock and designates one to have preference over the other in both dividend claim as well as claim against assets in the event of dissolution. The preferred with the first claim may be known as first claim preferred, or prior preferred, or senior preferred. Whatever terminology is used, it should be obvious which preferred has seniority. Remember, however, all preferred rank ahead of common stock, but **behind** debt securities.

SUMMARY

A corporation is the form of business best suited for raising significant sums of capital. It has two methods of doing so: equity and debt. Equity capital is raised through the issuance of stock. A corporation may not issue more shares than authorized by its charter. Common stockholders have many important legal rights, but they are not guaranteed a dividend. If the management of the corporation wishes, they may declare a dividend, usually quarterly and usually variable based on earnings. Sometimes a corporation pays the dividend in something other than cash, like stock (its own or any other stock it owns). Preferred stock is also ownership, it just has a prior claim on assets and earnings and has a fixed dividend. Also preferred stockholders must learn about and understand the terms: cumulative, convertible, callable, participating, and performance.

2

Debt Securities

"...In investing money, the amount of
interest you want, should
depend on whether you want to
eat well or to sleep well..."

J. Kenfield Morley
(1838-1923)
British Journalist

DEBT SECURITIES

As we discussed in the previous chapter, a corporation raises **capital** by issuing equity and debt securities. We have already covered equities, so in this chapter we will talk about **debt obligations**. It seems appropriate to begin once again with the basic question of: what is a bond? **A bond is a debt security which obligates the issuer to pay interest (usually semi-annually) and to repay the principal amount on the maturity date**. A bond represents a loan made to the issuer by an investor. When you buy a bond, you are lending the issuer money for a set period of time usually at a fixed annual rate of interest.

It is important to understand that when we talk about debt capital we are talking about **long-term** financing. Long-term debt, frequently called "funded debt" is money borrowed for a minimum period of five years, although more frequently the length of time is twenty to thirty years.

It is also important to know that there are three major issuers of debt.
1) Corporations
2) Local and State Governments
3) Federal Government

The largest issuer of debt securities (bonds) is the federal government. Bonds issued by the federal government or its agencies are referred to as "**Government Bonds**." Debt securities issued by state and local government are called "**Municipal Bonds.**" "Bonds issued by corporations are called, of course, "**Corporate Bonds**."

There are a few terms that are common to all debt securities.

Indenture   Frequently referred to as a deed of trust, the indenture details the terms of the legal agreement between the issuer and the investor. The indenture contains the duties and obligations of the trustee (usually a bank or trust company hired by the issuer) and all the rights of the bondholder, the lender.

Bearer   Sometimes referred to as **coupon** bonds, these bonds have interest "coupons" attached to each bond by the issuer. Since no name is on the bond or the coupon, whoever bears the bonds (has possession) is deemed the owner, hence the term bearer bonds. When the interest on the bond is due, the owner (bearer) clips a coupon off the bond and presents the coupon to the authorized bank for payment.

Bearer Bonds   Also the principal, when due, is payable to the holder (or bearer) of the bonds. The owner of a bearer bond should take great care of his/her bonds, if they are lost it is like losing cash. In fact, by the early 1980s, so much suspected illegal money was being laundered through the purchase of bearer bonds that Congress passed the Tax Act of 1982 which for all practical purposes, ended the issuance of bear bonds. There are still billions of dollars of coupon bonds in circulation, but none issued after 1982. Unless there is a change in the tax law, they will ultimately disappear altogether.

Registered   Most bonds sold today are delivered in fully registered form. When you buy these bonds they are registered in your name and every six months the issuer, or its trustee, sends the interest check to you, the registered owner. At the maturity date the principal is paid to the registered owner.

Book Entry   If you buy **government bonds**, and a growing number of other bonds, you will not receive bond certificates. By the middle of 1986, all marketable issues of the U S Treasury were issued in book entry form. This means that the owners of these securities do not actually possess any physical certificate; instead, a Federal Reserve Board computer keeps track of who owns what and when the interest should be paid. Book entry means, no certificate and no coupons.

The above three terms; bearer, registered, and book entry describe the different physical representations of bond ownership.

Other terms which are common to all bonds:

Par Value   Bonds are issued with a stated **par value** (usually $1000 minimum) and stated rate of interest on the debt. For example, suppose a $1000 par value bond is issued with a stated rate of interest of 8% by ABC Corporation in 1990. The maturity on the debt is 2010. ABC must pay $80 of interest annually to the bondholder for each of the 20 years the bond is outstanding.

Redemption   At maturity, ABC Corporation must repay the $1000 principal amount to the bondholder. The bond is **redeemed** by the issuer at **par**.

Zero-Coupon Bonds   Bonds can also be issued with a stated par value (usually $1000 minimum) but **without** a stated rate of interest. No semi-annual interest payments are made on "zero-coupon" bonds. Instead the bonds are purchased at a discount from par and are redeemed at par value on the maturity date.

Term Bonds   A bond issue where every bond has the **same interest rate and maturity** is called a term bond. Corporate bond issues and U.S. Government bond issues are typically term bonds.

Serial Bond   A bond issue with **differing maturities** is a serial bond issue. Because of the nature of interest rates, differing maturities require different interest rates. Thus, both maturities and interest rates differ for the bonds in the issue. Most municipal bonds issues are serial bonds.

Series Bonds   A bond issue where the bonds have the same maturity and different dates of issuance is a series bond issue. Series bonds are rarely issued, and are used to finance long-term construction projects where all of the money is not needed at once. Instead of floating a $10,000,000 bond issue today to build a new plant, a corporation might float a series bond issue, selling $5,000,000.00 of bonds this year, $3,000,000.00 next year, and $2,000,000.00 the following year, for a total issue of $10,000,000.00. By phasing in the bonds, the total interest cost to the issuer is reduced.

Bond Price Quotes

Term bonds (bonds that have the same interest rate and maturities) are quoted on a percentage of par basis. This is the same as quoting the bond on a dollar price basis.

Corporate Bonds   Corporate bonds are quoted as a percentage of par value, within minimum changes of 1/8 point.

For example, ABC Corporation debentures are quoted at 101 3/8. The dollar price of a $1000 par bond is 101.375 of $1000 par = $1013.75. (Remember: each bond point is worth $10.00)

Government Bonds   Government bonds are quoted as a percentage of par value, with minimum changes of 1/32 point.

For example, a U.S. Treasury Bond is quoted at 99.24. The dollar price of a $1000 par bond is 99 and 24/32 % of par = 99 and .75 % = 99.75% of $1000 par = $997.50.

Municipal Bonds   Municipal bond issues are generally serial bonds. As previously stated, serial bonds have different maturities and different interest rates. This means that each maturity has a different value, and therefore, a different market price. It would be very cumbersome to quote different market prices for each maturity within an issue. Instead, serial bonds are quoted on a "yield basis," also known as a basis quote. A basis quote is is given in "basis points."

Basis Points   A quote of 5.50 is a bond priced to yield 5.50%. One basis point equals .01% on a bond. Ten basis points equals .1%. One hundred basis points equals one full point or 1%.

The Effect of Interest Rates on Bond Prices

Par Value   When a bond sells in the market for the same price as its par value (usually $1000) the bond is said to be selling at **par**.

Discount Bond   When a bond is selling below its stated par value, the bond is said to be selling at a **discount**.

For example, a $1000 par corporate bond quoted at 90 is selling at a discount of 10 points ($100) from par. (Remember: each bond point equals $10)

Premium Bond   Also, when a bond is selling above its stated par value, it is said to be selling at a **premium**.

For example, a $1000 par corporate is quoted at 110 is selling at a premium of 10 points ($100) over par.

Interest Rates Up Bond Prices Down   Assume that a bond has a coupon of 5.50%. As long as interest rates in general remain the same, the market price of this bond will remain at par. But happens if interest rates in general rise? Well, lets assume general interest rates were 5.50% when this bond was issued, but now rates have risen to 6.00%. If you were buying a bond which bond would you buy? The old bond yielding 5.50%, or the new bonds being issued at 6.00%. Of course, most investors would buy the higher yielding bond. Therefore, to be competitive in the marketplace, the price of the 5.50% bonds must drop to a level which produces 6.00% yield. Hence, our first bond law: **When interest rates rise, bond prices must fall**.

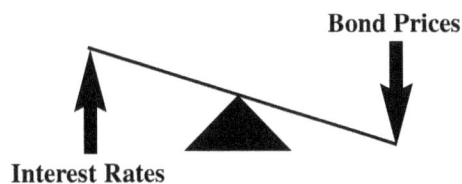

Interest Rates Down Bond Prices Up On the other hand, what happens if interest rates fall in general? Assume that interest rates in general fall to 5%. Our bond yields 5.50% if it is priced at par. To be competitive with the market, the price of our bond will rise to a level where the yields equals 5%. Therefore our second law; when interest rates fall, the price of bonds must rise.

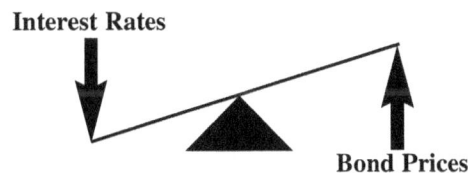

To summarize, when interest rates rise, bond prices fall. When interest rates fall, bond prices rise. This is known as the inverse relationship between bond prices and interest rates.

Bond Prices Other factors effecting bond prices are, maturity and coupon rates. As interest rates move, bond prices do not move in equal amounts. The longer the bonds maturity, the faster the bond's price will move in response to interest rate changes. Conversely, the shorter the bond's maturity, the slower its price move, with respect to interest rates. This maturity relationship is due to the compounding effect of interest rates on the bond's value.

Bond Prices Another factor effecting bond prices is the coupon rate. The lower the coupon rate on a given bond, the greater the price volatility of that bond in response to interest rate movements. Bonds with low coupon rates tend to trade at discounts; therefore, discount bond prices move more rapidly in response to interest rate movements than do premium bond prices.

Bond Yields

There are three basic yields that bond investors should be not only be familiar with, but also know how to calculate. They are:
   1) Nominal Yield
   2) Current Yield
   3) Yield To Maturity

Assume that a corporate bond dealer is offering a 10 year, 10% bond at 90. This bond is being offered at a discount, therefore, the true yield of the bond is higher than the stated yield. The three yields are as follows:

Nominal Yield This is the simplest and most straight forward. The nominal yield is nothing more than the bond's stated rate of interest, also sometimes referred to as the coupon rate. In the above example, the nominal yield is, that's right, 10%.

Current Yield The current yield takes into account the market price of the bond. If this bond were selling at par (100), the current yield would be the same as the nominal yield.

However, since this bond is trading at a discount (90), the current yield has to be the 10% nominal yield **PLUS** a little extra. The formula for calculating the current yield is as follows:

$$\text{Current Yield} = \frac{\text{Annual Interest In Dollars}}{\text{Bond Market Price}}$$

Still using our example above, the current yield for this bond is:

$$\frac{\$100}{\$900} = 11.11\%$$

Please note that the current yield is higher than the nominal yield, this is because of the discounted price of the bond.

Yield To Maturity

Yield to maturity takes into account both the market price of the bond as well as any capital gains or losses on the bond if held to maturity. This calculation, while it does posses a few more twist and turns, is still rather straight forward and not at all difficult. The formula is as follows:

Yield To Maturity =

Annual Income + Annual Capital Gain (Discount Bond)
            - Annual Capital Loss (Premium Bond)
_____

Average Price = Purchase Price + Redemption Price

2

In our example, the yield to maturity for this bond is:

$$\frac{\dfrac{\$100 + \$10}{\dfrac{\$900 + \$1000}{2}}}{}$$ $100 discount over 10 years= $10 year

$$\frac{\$110}{\$950} = 11.58\%$$

Note the yield to maturity is higher than current yield, this is due to the inclusion of capital gains arising from the discounted bond purchase price. It is also important to understand the converse relationship. If this bond had been purchased at a premium, the current yield would be lower than the nominal yield, and the yield to maturity would be lower than the current yield. This is illustrated in our next example.

For this example lets assume a 10 year, 10% corporate bond quoted at 110.

Nominal Yield $=$ 10% (easy enough)

Current Yield $= \dfrac{\text{Annual Interest In Dollars}}{\text{Bond's Market Price}}$

$$= \frac{\$100}{\$110} = 9.09\%$$

Yield To Maturity $= \dfrac{\text{Annual Income} + \text{Annual Capital Gain} - \text{Annual Capital Loss}}{\text{Average Price} = \dfrac{\text{Purchase Price} + \text{Redemption Price}}{2}}$

$$= \frac{\$100 - \$10}{\dfrac{\$1100 + \$1000}{2}}$$

$$= \frac{\$90}{\$1050} = 8.57\%$$

As stated earlier, these are the 3 basic types of bond yields. You should be able to define, understand, and, if necessary, calculate each yield.

Risk Associated With Bonds

Bondholders are subject to a variety of risk. An evaluation of a bond should take into consideration the risks associated with bonds. These risks are:

Credit Risk
Credit risk is the risk that the issuer cannot make interest and principal payments on an issue. Rating agencies rate bonds only for credit risk, not for any other type of risk.

There are two primary rating agencies. They are Moody's and Standard and Poors. Government Bonds are not rated because they are considered to have no credit risk. They have the highest credit rating. Long term corporate and municipal bonds are rated under the "ABC" system.

The ratings used by the two agencies for long term bonds are:

	Standard and Poors	Moodys
Investment Grade	AAA AA A BB	Aaa Aa A Baa
Speculative Grade	BB B CCC CC C	Ba B Caa Ca C

Investment Grade

The top 4 ratings are considered "investment" grade. The highest investment grade is AAA, while the lowest is BBB. Generally, institutions will restrict their bond investments to those of investment grades only.

Speculative Grade ("Junk")

Any bonds not receiving a rating high enough to be considered investment grade are termed: Speculative Grade. Speculative bonds are commonly referred to as "junk bonds." Thus, a BB rated bond is the highest "junk rating" available.

Standard and Poor's can adjust a rating slightly without making a letter change by adding a "+", or "-" to the rating. For example, a A+ rating is better than a A rating. For Moody's, it adjust ratings by adding "1, 2, 3,". For example, a A-1 rating is higher than a A-2 rating; and A-2 is higher than a A-3 rating and so on.

Other Bond Risks

Interest Rate Risk

The risk that rising interest rates will cause bond prices to fall. Long term maturities, low coupon rate bonds and deep discount bonds are most susceptible to interest rate risk as discussed previously in this chapter.

Purchasing Power Risk The risk that inflation will lower the value of bond interest payments and principal repayment, thereby forcing prices to fall.

Marketability Risk The risk that the security will be difficult to sell. Many factors affect marketability, including but not limited to; the issue's size, the number of traders in the market, general market conditions.

Liquidity Risk The risk that the security can only be sold by incurring large transaction cost. Generally, short term higher quality issues are liquid; the longer the term and lower the quality, the lessor the liquidity.

Legislative Risk The risk that new laws reduce the value of a security, such as a change in the tax laws increasing tax rates on interest received from bonds.

Call Risk The risk that the bonds may be redeemed prior to maturity, forcing reinvestment of the proceeds at a lower interest rate. Call risk increases as interest rates fall in the market, since issuers are able to call in existing higher rate issues and refinance at lower current market rates.

Reinvestment Risk The risk that, as payments are received from an investment, interest rates have fallen. When the funds are reinvested, the investor receives a lower yield.

The preceding section of this chapter has dealt primarily with generalities that are basic to most bond investments. For the remainder of this chapter, we will briefly discuss some specifics related to each of the 3 major debt issuers. As mentioned earlier, the three primary types of debt are:

    1) Corporate Debt
    2) Government Debt
    3) Municipal Debt

CORPORATE DEBT

Corporations issue debt in order to raise capital. The debt can take the form of long-term bonds, intermediate term notes, or short term notes known as commercial paper.

Notes and Bonds Fully Registered

Commercial Paper

Intermediate and long term bonds are typically issued in fully registered form. This means that the bondholder is registered with the transfer agent as the owner of record and a physical certificate is issued to the bondholder. Short tern commercial paper is issued in **book entry form**. This means, no physical certificates are issued, but the holders name and address, and purchase amount are registered on the "**books**" of the transfer agent.

Transfer Agent

Paying Agent

The transfer agent keeps the record of the owners of the outstanding debt, and when the debt is traded, "transfers" the ownership record to the new owner. The same financial institution usually acts as the paying agent for the issuer as well. The paying agent actually makes the interest payments to the owners of record and handles debt redemptions.

Trust Indenture

The bonds are issued under a contract called an "**indenture**". The indenture specifically states all the relevant features of the bonds. For example, the indenture will states the interest rate, maturity, collateral, and call provisions as well as any other specifics deemed relevant to the bond issue. The indenture may also call for the issuer to maintain specific protections for the bondholders such as insurance coverage, audit by independent accountant, and certain ratios of assets to liabilities.

To insure that the corporation adheres to the indenture, an independent trustee is appointed to monitor compliance with the provisions of the indenture. The trustee reports annually to the bondholders, and is expected to inform the bondholders if he finds noncompliance. The trustee is usually a commercial bank. All corporate issues of $5,000,000.00 or more must have a Trust Indenture as specified by the Trust Indenture Act of 1939.

Secured and Unsecured Corporate Debt

Corporate bonds can be secured or unsecured. When a bond is secured, specific collateral is pledged to back the bond issue. If the corporation defaults, the bondholders have claim to the collateral. Because of the extra protection afforded by the collateral, secured bonds can be sold at lower rates than unsecured bonds. Secured bonds are typically long-term maturities. These bonds are:

Mortgage Bond Real Estate such as a factory is pledged as collateral for the bond issue. The bondholder has a lien on the property and therefrom a right to sell the mortgaged real estate if the bondholders claims are not satisfied. Mortgage Bonds are the most common form of corporate debt, and are the principal financing source for public utilities.

Open End If the trust indenture is open-end, the corporation can sell additional bonds having equal status against the real estate. However, open-end trust indentures usually include an "additional bonds test" requirement which means that before additional bonds can be issued, the corporation must show that it will be able to meet the additional interest and principal expense.

Closed End If the trust indenture is closed end, new bonds can be issued only if they are **junior** (have lower status in a liquidation) to the existing bonds.

Equipment Trust Certificate

Equipment owned by the corporation is pledged as collateral. This is the typical form of financing for common carriers such as airlines, trucking companies, and railroads. For example, if an airline wanted to buy new planes, it could finance the purchase by issuing equipment trust certificates. The planes are the collateral backing the issue. Equipment trust certificates are issued in serial form (unlike most other corporate debts which are term issues). Serial bonds obligate the issuer to repay a portion of principal each year until the bonds are retired. In effect, the equipment is bought under a "pay-as-you use it" plan. The life of the issue coincides with the equipment's life.

Collateral Trust Certificates

A portfolio of marketable securities placed in trust as collateral. The typical use of this type of financing is when a parent company pledges the securities of a subsidiary as collateral.

Unsecured Corporate Debt

Unsecured corporate debt is simply backed by the issuer's promise to pay. There is no collateral backing the issue. Unsecured debt is issued in short term, intermediate term, and long term maturities.

Commercial Paper

Very short-term corporate financing needs are met by issuing commercial paper. Maturities usually range from 14 to 90 days, with 30 days being the most common maturity. The security will never exceed 270 days because the issue would then have to be registered with the SEC, and expensive and time consuming process.

Discount Instrument

Because of the short-term nature, obviously semi-annual interest payments cannot be made as with longer term debt. Instead, commercial paper is sold at a discount and matures at face value. The difference is the earned interest income, which is effectively received at maturity. Unlike longer term debt sold in $1000 units, commercial paper is sold in large units, - $100,000 up to $1,000,000 per certificate.

Book Entry Commercial paper is sold in book entry form. The purchasers are large institutions with excess cash to invest. There is very limited trading of these instruments–most investors simply hold them to maturity.

Debentures Intermediate and long term corporate debt is backed solely by the full faith and credit of the issuer. There is no collateral backing the issue. Debentures are issued by "blue chip" corporations with high credit ratings who do not have to back the issue with assets. Lower credit rated issuers also issue debentures in the form of high yield or "junk bonds." Compared to a secured bond, credit risk is higher for a debenture holder.

Subordinated Debentures Debentures can also be issued as "subordinated" debt. Holders of subordinated debentures agree to a lower status in corporate liquidations. If a corporation becomes insolvent, subordinated debt holders are paid after senior creditors. In order to entice investors to buy subordinated debt, something extra is generally given to compensate for assumption of this incremental risk. This "something extra" could be a higher interest rate, or it could take the form of a "**conversion feature**." This feature allows the bondholder to convert the bonds into a specific number of common shares. The conversion feature of these bonds could prove to be very valuable to the investor as it allows the bondholder to participate, to a certain degree, in the appreciation of the common stock price, should there be any. Usually one or both of these "**sweeteners**" is inducement enough for bond investors.

Income Bonds   When a corporation goes bankrupt, the issuer defaults on its outstanding debt. The company then attempts to reorganize and emerge from bankruptcy. Part of the reorganization is to get existing bondholders to give up any claims they have under the old issue and to accept new bonds in their place. This new bond is termed an "**income bond**" because it obligates the issuer to pay only if the corporation has sufficient "income" or earnings. The bondholders are likely to accept this new bond instrument since they are receiving nothing anyway. To induce the bondholders to accept the new issue, they are often given a greater principal amount than they had before. Therefore, the principal amount is "adjusted" on

Adjustment Bonds   these bonds, hence, they are also referred to as "**adjustment bonds**."

Income Bonds Trade Flat   Interest accrues on the bonds but it is only paid if the corporation returns to profitability. In theory, if the corporation is profitable, all missed interest payments will be made up. Because these bonds are not currently paying interest, they are said to be trading "**flat**" in the in the market. Any bond which does not pay interest trades "**flat**."

Convertible Debentures   Convertible bonds are corporate debentures which can be converted, at the option of the owner, into the common stock of the issuer. At the time of issuance, a conversion price is set per share. The bond can then be converted, based on its par value, into a fixed number of common shares.

At the time of issuance, the conversion price is set at a premium to the stock's current market price. In order for the conversion feature to benefit the bondholder, the stock's price must rise above the conversion price.

Corporate Debt Retirement Provisions

Retiring Debt

Corporate bonds may be redeemed at maturity, or, if a call provision is included in the Trust Indenture, may be "called" under the terms of the provision. In this manner debt is retired. The indenture can also call for the estab-

Sinking Fund

lishment of a "**sinking fund**." A sinking fund is an account or fund that is set up so that money is deposited by the corporation periodically (usually annually), and the funds are used to retire the bonds at maturity or to retire a portion of the issue each year after a specified date. The sinking fund is an extra protection measure for bondholders. The terms of the sinking fund usually allow the issuer to retire portions of the issue by either calling the bonds or buying them in the open market if the price is lower than the call price.

Refunding Debt

Instead of retiring debt, a corporation may simply roll it over in part or in full. It does this by issuing a refunding bond issue and using the proceeds to retire or call debt. A corporation issues refunding bonds when interest rates have dropped (to retire expensive debt and replace it with lower interest rate or "cheaper" debt) or when it simply does not have the funds or the desire to retire bonds.

Trading of Corporate Debt

Corporate debt is traded on both the over-the-counter market, and the New York Stock Exchange.

Over the Counter Trading

Most corporate debt is traded in the over-the-counter market. This is a dealer-to-dealer market, with trading conducted over the phone. There is no electronic trading system for corporate bonds as there is for stocks because trading volume is comparatively light. A round lot trade of bonds is five $1000 par value bonds. ($5000 face amount). Corporate bond prices are quoted through

Yellow Sheets sheets of paper termed "**Yellow Sheets**". These yellow sheets are published daily (They are actually yellow).

Settlement and Accrued Interest

Regular Way Corporate bond trades settle "regular way" unless special delivery terms are required. A regular way trade settles three business days after the trade date.

Cash If a seller does not want to wait for a number of business days to be paid , the trade can be done "for cash". Cash settlement occurs the same day before 2:30 PM. The downside for the seller is, to induce someone to pay today, the bonds would have to be sold at a lower price than in a regular way trade.

Accrued Interest When a bond trade settles, the buyer must pay to the seller the purchase price of the bond plus any commissions due to the broker. In addition, the seller is entitled to any interest on the bond during the period that it has been held between interest payment dates. When the bond changes hands, the ownership is changed with the transfer agent. The new holder of the bond will receive the entire 6-month interest payment on the due date. Because the new owner is not entitled to the entire 6-month interest payment, the investor must pay the previous owner his/her pro rata share.

U.S. Government Debt

Characteristics of U.S. Government Debt

Largest Debt Market The U.S. Government issues debt in order to finance the continuous operations of the government. The market for U.S. Government debt is one of the largest and most active trading markets in the world. Currently, there is almost **6 trillion** in government debt outstanding (our accumulated federal deficit). Negotiable government debt issues take the form of long-term bonds, intermediate-term notes and short-term notes known as Treasury Bills.

Savings Bond

Savings bonds are **NOT** part of this market–they are non-negotiable securities and therefore cannot be traded in the open market. They are purchased from the government and can only be redeemed by the government.

New Issues Book Entry

Short-term Treasury Bills, intermediate-term notes and long term bonds are typically issued in "book entry" form. No certificates are issued for book entry securities. The only ownership record is the "book" of owners kept by the transfer agent. No physical certificates have been issued since 1983. Prior to that date, notes and bonds were available in physical certificate form. These outstanding securities continue to trade until their redemption date.

Sold At Auction

U.S. Government debt is sold by competitive bidding at a weekly auction conducted by the Federal Reserve. At the weekly auctions, Treasury Bills are sold. Every four weeks, notes and bonds are sold.

Agency Debt

Debt is also issued by agencies of the U.S. Government While Treasury debt is backed directly by the U.S. Governments' promise to pay, Agency debt is not. Agency debt is backed by the "implicit promise" to pay if the issuing agency should default. All U.S. Government debt is considered to be the highest rated debt on the open market; due primarily to the governments ability to tax coupled with the fact that the U.S.

Government has never defaulted on a debt issue. However, agency debt is considered to be slightly less safe than direct Treasury debt.

U.S. GOVERNMENT OBLIGATIONS

Treasury Bonds

Treasury Bonds are long-term securities issued with maturities ranging from over 10 to 30 years. These bonds are issued in multiples of $1000 par value and pay interest semi-annually to registered holders. Treasury bonds are quoted as a percentage of par value in 32nds. Long Treasury Bonds are usually callable 5 years prior to maturity. If rates have dropped, the Treasury could then call in these issues prior to maturity.

Treasury Notes

Treasury Notes are intermediate term securities issued with maturities ranging from over 1 to 10 years. The notes are issued in multiples of $1000 par value and pay interest semi-annually to registered holders. Treasury notes are quoted as a percentage of par value in 32nds. Notes are non-callable.

Treasury Bills

Treasury Bills are short term securities issued with 3, 6, and 12 month maturities. Treasury Bills are issued at a discount to par ($10,000 minimum) and mature at par. The discount earned is considered to be the interest income. They are quoted on a discount yield basis.

TRADING OF GOVERNMENT/AGENCY DEBT

Over the Counter Trading

Trading of government and agency securities takes place exclusively in the over the counter market. There is no trading on **any** exchange floor. The participants in the market include large commercial banks, foreign banks, U.S. Government securities dealers, brokerage firms, as well as the Federal Reserve itself.

Primary Dealers

The largest participants in the government market are U.S. Government securities dealers. There are about 45 firms which have primary dealer status. The Federal Reserve designates a dealer as a primary dealer after the firm demonstrates over many years its ability to purchase Treasury securities at the weekly auction and to make an orderly trading market in those issues (that is, the ability to resell them to the public). Primary dealers are connected to the Federal Reserve wire system and deal directly with the "Fed."

Secondary Dealers

All other firms trading U.S. Government securities are termed "secondary" dealers. These firms buy and sell Treasuries in the market through the primary dealers, but are permitted to bid in the weekly auction. Most smaller banks and brokerage firms are "secondary" dealers.

Federal Reserve as a Dealer

The Federal Reserve maintains its own trading account and buys and sells large quantities of government securities in the market to manage interest rates. This activity is called "**Open Market Operations**."

Quotations

Quotes for U.S. Government issues are placed by the primary dealers on a computer quotation system through services such as Bloomberg, Reuters and Telerate. Paper quote sheets (like the Yellow Sheets for corporate bonds) are obsolete because trading in these securities is so active.

Settlement of Government and Agency Securities

Regular Way

Trades of U.S.Government securities (Treasury Bills, Notes and Bonds) settle "regular way," that is on the first business day after trade date ("regular way" for US Gov't. securities is 1 business day).

Trades of Agency Securities that pay interest semi-annually generally settle regular way. However, Agency settlement dates do vary. To find the exact settlement date of a particular agency security, one should consult the Public Securities Association or ones stockbroker.

MUNICIPAL DEBT

Characteristics of Municipal Debt

Municipal Bonds

Municipal bonds are debt issues of state and local governments, territories, and political subdivisions. A principal feature of municipal debt is the tax status of the interest income. Generally, it is exempt from Federal income tax, but subject to state and local tax. However, there is another tax benefit of municipal securities. Most states, in an effort to keep local money at home, have enacted legislation which makes interest income on municipal securities **exempt from local and state tax also**, if the purchasers are residents of the issuers state or local municipality.

Fully Registered

Currently, virtually all new municipal debt is issued in fully registered form, meaning the name of the owner is registered with the transfer agent and a certificate is issued to the purchaser. Interest payments are mailed directly to the bondholder of record from the transfer agent. At redemption, the bondholder surrenders the certificate to obtain repayment of principal.

Book-Entry Form

Some years ago, a few municipalities tried to market municipal issues in book-entry form. No certificates were issued; instead the only ownership record is on the transfer agents books. These issues met with great customer resistance and were not successful. Recently there has been some movement back in this direction, mainly in the area of "short term municipal notes," but comparatively few municipal issues are sold "book-entry."

Bearer Form

Until mid-1983, most municipal bonds were issued in bearer form. Bearer certificates are simply engraved "payable to bearer"–there is no record of the owners name on the bond or on the transfer agents books. Bearer bonds have coupons attached (also payable to the bearer) which are clipped every 6 months and submitted to the transfer agent for payment. Bearer bonds are very desirable to individuals who do not want others (like the IRS) to know what assets they have. Because of this, Congress prohibited municipal bearer bonds in 1983. Because bearer bonds are more desirable than fully registered bonds, they trade at higher prices. Thus, the municipal market is said to be "two-tiered."

Legal Opinion

All municipal issues must have a legal opinion printed on the face of the bond. Before a bond can be issued, the municipality retains a bond counsel. The bond counsel examines the issue to make sure it is legally binding on the issuer, is valid, and that the interest is exempt from Federal tax under current law. The bond counsel prepares all the legal documentation necessary for the issue and renders an opinion. Issuers desire an "**unqualified legal opinion**." Such an opinion means the bond counsel finds that everything is "OK," and that there are no problems with the issue. If the counsel does find a problem, he "qualifies" the opinion, stating that there is a legal uncertainty of which any purchaser should be aware.

Serial Bonds

Municipalities issue long-term debt and short term notes. Most long term bonds are "serial maturities"–meaning the maturities are spread over a sequence of years. These bonds are issued at par and pay interest semi-annually.

Short-term notes are issued at a discount from par and mature at par value.

Municipal issues are broadly characterized into 4 types of bonds;

1) General Obligation Bonds
2) Revenue Bonds
3) Special Types of Bonds
4) Short Term Notes

General Obligation Bonds

General Obligations

A general obligation bond is backed by the full faith, credit and taxing power of the issuer. The type of taxes which back general obligation bonds depends on the issuing entity. Local governments have the ability to collect property taxes, known as "Ad Valorem" taxes. Local governments usually do not collect income taxes. Therefore, local governmental issues are usually backed by "unlimited" ad Valorem taxes. This means that the issuer (town or city) promises to raise taxes without any limit in order to pay off the bondholders. In some cases, local issuers will sell bonds backed by "limited" taxing power. This means that the amount of taxing power to pay the bonds has a defined maximum amount.

Limited Tax Bonds

Revenue Bonds

Revenue Bond

A revenue bond is one backed by a specific source of revenue. The full faith and credit of the issuer is not pledged. Since only the specific revenues of a particular project back a revenue bond, the bond is said to be a self-supporting debt.

Feasibility Study
Because the bond issue is backed solely by the project's future revenues, it is extremely important to insure that the project is viable. That is, that the actual revenues will be able to service and retire the bond issue. Therefore all revenue bond issues are required to have a feasibility study completed. The feasibility study is usually prepared by outside consultants, who do not have a vested interest (supposedly) in seeing the project approved.

Special Types of Municipal Debt

The two largest types of municipal offerings are revenue bonds and general obligation bonds. Revenue bonds make up approximately 50% of municipal issues and General Obligation bonds make up about 35%. The rest of the municipal bond market is comprised of "special" types of bonds. Because these "special" type issues make up such a small percent of the overall municipal bond market, we will review just briefly on the various types.

Special Tax
An issue secured by a tax other than an ad valorem tax, usually an excise tax such as cigarette, liquor, gasoline, etc.

Special Assessment
An issue secured by a special assessment on a particular segment of the municipality. For example, new street lights may be put in one area, and only that area is assessed higher taxes to pay for the improvement.

Moral Obligation
A bond issue which is backed **only** by the issuers "**promise**" to repay, but not the legal obligation to repay. Usually, this type of bond is issued only in times of distress and carries a higher level of credit risk.

Double Barreled
An issue backed by a revenue source other than Ad Valorem taxes but also backed by the faith, credit and

taxing power of a municipal issuer. For example, a housing bond (revenue) may be backed as well by the issuer's Ad Valorem taxing power to improve its credit rating. This type of bond is treated as a General Obligation bond since the ultimate source of payment is taxing power.

New Housing Authority   New / Public Housing Authority Bonds (also called PHA or Section 8 bonds) are used to finance the construction of subsidized housing. This type of issue is backed by the rents, U.S. Government subsidies, and by the faith, credit and taxing power of the U.S. Government. While PHAs are backed by two sources of income, they do not meet the industry definition of a double-barreled issue since they are backed by Federal taxing power, **not** municipal taxing power. These bonds are no longer issued; however, there are outstanding issues that still trade.

Lease Rental   An issue used to finance office construction where the user is a state or city agency. The rents paid by the user are the revenue source and the user is generally obligated to to appropriate the funds for the lease payments from general tax revenues.

Industrial Development Bond   Industrial Development Bonds are issued by a state, city, or local agency to build an industrial facility that is leased to a private company. The lease payments of the company are the revenue source. IDBs are also guaranteed by the private user; take on its credit rating; and are considered the user's liability-not the issuer's.

Short Term Municipal Notes

Municipalities issue short term notes, usually 12 month maturities, although they may be issued for as short as 3 months or as long as 3 years. Short term notes are used for 2 general purposes;

1) For temporary financing of capital improvement

2) To even out cash flows

Short-term notes can be categorized in primarily 2 types. The first type is used to obtain short-term financing for a building project, to be replaced by permanent financing at the completion of the project. These are:

1) BANs - Bond Anticipation Notes

2) CLNs - Construction Loan Notes

The second type of municipal short term note is used to "pull forward" an income source and the use of monies before they are actually collected. These are:

1) TANs - Tax Anticipation Notes

2) RANs - Revenue Anticipation Notes

3)TRANs - Tax and Revenue Anticipation Notes

TRADING OF MUNICIPAL DEBT

Muncipal Trading

Trading in the municipal bond market is very limited. All trades take place in the over the counter market. This thin market is generally caused by the triple taxation factor of municipal securities. In effect, the municipal market is a state by state market. People in California buy California bonds, not New York bonds; and people in New York buy New York bonds, not California bonds.

Blue List

Municipal bond price quotes are published daily on sheets of paper referred to in the industry as "Blue Sheets". These sheets are actually "blue" and are distributed to subscribing dealers daily.

Firm or Nominal Bid

Municipal trading terminology is a bit unusual, to accommodate the fact that the market is quite illiquid and not actively traded. A dealer "**bidding**" for a bond is willing to buy at the stated price or yield. A "**firm**" quote means the dealer will honor that price. If the quote is "**nominal**," the dealer is giving an idea of the price, not an actual price.

TAX STATUS OF MUNICIPAL DEBT INTEREST

Since municipal interest is federally tax free, it is necessary to utilize 2 formulas to accurately compare taxable issues with municipals.

These formulas are:
1) Tax Equivalent Yield
2) Tax Free Equivalent Yield

Tax Equivalent Yield
$$TEY = \frac{\text{Municipal Yield}}{100\% - \text{investor tax bracket}}$$

For example, a municipal bond with a coupon rate of 7% when purchased at par, by an investor in the 30% tax bracket; what will will be the tax equivalent yield?

$$TEY = \frac{7}{100-30} = \frac{7}{70} = .10\%$$

The tax equivalent yield on this municipal bond is 10 percent.

The tax free equivalent yield is used to calculate just the reverse of the above. It is used to convert a taxable yield (corporate or Treasury) to a non-taxable yield (municipal). The formula is:

Tax Free Equivalent Yield = Taxable Yield x (100% - Tax Bracket)

For example, a customer in the 25% tax bracket is considering buying a 10% corporate bond or a 8% municipal bond.

	=	10%	x	(100 - 25)
	=	10%	x	.75
Tax Free Equivalent	=	7.5%
Yield		

Since the tax free equivalent yield of the corporate bond is 7.5 percent, the investor would obviously choose the higher yielding municipal security. These formulas prove invaluable in evaluating taxable versus non-taxable interest income securities.

3

Money Markets

"...To be conscious that you are
ignorant of the facts is a great
step to knowledge..."

Benjamin Disraeli
(1804-81)
British novelist and prime minister

MONEY MARKET DEBT

Characteristics of Money Market Instruments

Definition   When we talk about stocks and bonds, we are talking about securities that are traded in the capital markets, that is, the market for long-term capital. What then, is the money market? The money market is... "the market for buying and selling short-term loanable funds in the form of securities and loans." It is called the money market because that is what is traded there,...money.

Matures 1 Year or Less   While there are many different kinds of money instruments, they have several common factors. A money market instrument is a debt obligation which matures in 1 year or less. In fact, the majority of money market instruments mature in less than six months. Because of the short maturity, the instrument will be turned into money very soon, hence the name money market.

Issued at Discount   A second factor that most (but not all) money market instruments share is that they are issued at a discount, that is, they do not pay interest.

Safety   A third factor shared by money market instruments is their safety. While some are not quite as safe as others, (commercial paper is not as safe as Treasury bills) they are all considered to be "low risk" securities.

Types of Money Market Instruments

Treasury Bills   Treasury Bills are the largest money market instrument and are considered to be the bellwether of the money market. Other Treasury securities also trade in the money

Notes & Bonds   market. **Any Treasury securities** (Treasury Notes and Bonds) which has 12 months or less to its maturity date, is considered a money market instrument.

Treasury Security Advantages

No Risk There are a number of advantages to purchasing Treasury securities as opposed to other money market instruments. First, and foremost, is the complete absence of business risk (sometimes called financial or credit risk). It is just inconceivable (or at least most seem to think) that the U.S. Government would be unable to pay-off its financial obligations due within the next 12 months.

High Liquidity A second advantage is the extremely high liquidity in the secondary markets. In all securities markets, inactive securities have a wider "bid - ask" spread than active securities. Hence, the more active a security, the narrower the spread. The huge market activity in Treasury securities keeps the spreads very low, making it easy for investors to get in and out at a reasonable cost.

Tax Exempt A third benefit of investing in Treasuries is that the interest is **exempt from state income tax**. Because of all of these factors, yields on treasuries are normally the lowest in the money market.

Other Money Market Securities

Federal Funds Do not confuse Treasury securities with Federal funds. Federal funds have nothing to do with the Federal government. Federal Reserve member banks are required to hold a portion of their total deposits with the Federal Reserve. Occasionally, some banks have more on deposit than required by law. When this occurs, these banks are said to have "**excess reserves**". Also, there are occasions where banks find themselves in a deficit reserve situation. You should now be able to guess what happens. Member banks with excess reserves lend these reserves to member banks with deficits. These loans are very short term, usually only overnight. These funds can only be exchanged between members of the Federal Reserve, hence the term Federal Funds. This lending from one bank to another is known as federal funds lending and is done so at a rate of interest which is called the **federal fund rate**.

Commercial Paper

Commercial paper represents short-term IOUs issued by corporations, generally in minimum denominations of $100,000 and sold to public and institutional investors alike. Most commercial paper is issued by finance companies or major industrial organizations. The largest finance company is GMAC. Ford and GE are also major finance company issuers of commercial paper. Commercial paper has a maximum maturity of 270 days since any longer maturity would require the expense of filing with the SEC. Commercial paper is almost always issued at a discount, and hence, pays no interest.

Bankers Acceptances

Bankers acceptances are used to finance import/export businesses. They also are issued at a discount and mature within no more than 270 days as well. They are used extensively in international trade. They are termed bankers acceptances because banks accept the responsibility to pay the balances owed.

Negotiable Certificates of Deposit

Certificates of deposits are unsecured time deposits, which usually pay a fixed rate of interest. CDs do not pay periodic interest; interest is paid in full at maturity. To be considered a negotiable CD, such CDs must have a face value of at least $100,000 or more, with 1 million dollars and upwards being most prevalent. While most CDs have an original maturity of one to three months, there is no time limit and CDs of 3 to 5 years duration are not uncommon.

Repurchase Agreements

Repurchase agreements are agreements between buyers and seller to reverse a trade at a specified time at a specified yield. In effect, a security is created, collateralized by underlying U.S. Government securities and any other eligible security. In the marketplace, repurchase agreements are usually referred to as "**repos**." The most common term of repurchase agreements is overnight. These overnight repos have virtually no risk and therefore carry slightly lower yields than other money market instruments.

Eurodollars

A **Eurodollar** is a U.S. dollar which is used primarily in Europe....right? WRONG!! If there was ever a money market instrument that was misnamed it's the Eurodollar. Eurodollar is merely the term given to represent **U.S. Dollar denominated deposits in foreign banks**, whether they be in Europe, the Far East, or South America. These deposits of millions of dollars, residing in foreign banks, denominated in U.S. dollars, represent a source of short term money for corporations worldwide. Foreign banks trade these funds similar to the domestic trading of Fed Funds. Domestic banks with a reserve deficiency can borrow "Euro's" as a substitute for Fed Funds. The difference is that Fed funds are loaned overnight - Euro's can be loaned for longer periods ranging from 1 day to 5 years. These longer terms allow U.S. banks greater flexibility in meeting there reserve requirements.

LIBOR

The interest rate charged on Eurodollar loans between major international banks is "**LIBOR**" - the London Interbank Offered Rate. "**LIBOR**" is the average offered rate for Eurodollar loans of 5 major banks centered in London.

4

Mutual Funds

"...The man who does not read good books, has no advantage over the man who can't read them..."

Mark Twain
(1835-1910)
American author

MUTUAL FUNDS

Most of you have heard the term "mutual fund", but really, what are they? How did they come to be? How are they traded? How are they priced? And what rights do you have as a shareholder and owner? These questions, along with other items of importance are the focus of this section.

Investment Company
A mutual fund is, by definition, an investment company. An investment company is an entity that collects money from individuals, pools it, and invests those funds in a manner consistent with the common objective(s) of the participants. While the term "mutual fund" is widely known and recognized, the technically correct term would be "management company."

The Investment Company Act of 1940 created the categories and regulates the functions of investment companies. The act created three basic types of investment companies. They are:

1) Face Amount Certificate Companies
2) Unit Investment Trust
3) Management Companies
    A) Open-End
    B) Closed End

Face Amount Certificate
"Face Amount Certificate," virtually obsolete today, is a certificate issued in a certain maturing "face amount", and requires the purchaser to make monthly installments. Over the course of the term, the monthly payment and the interest would pay to the purchaser the stated "face amount" of the certificate. This definition is just for a historical perspective. Today these certificates are virtually nonexistent.

Unit Investment Trust

A "unit investment trust" is a company which is established by a trust indenture. That means the company is not incorporated. Incorporated companies issue "shares," while trust companies issue "shares of beneficial interest." These shares represent an interest in specific "units"of securities.

Management Companies

A management company is an investment company chartered as a corporation and issuing shares of stock. The management company professionally manages a portfolio of securities for its shareholders. As you can see from our brief review of investment companies, what the world has come to know as "mutual funds," are really **management companies**. For our purposes, and for sake of clarity and simplicity, we will utilize the term "mutual fund" for this text.

As noted earlier, there are two types of mutual funds, **open end** and **closed end**.

Open End Fund

What would you guess is the distinguishing characteristic of the "open" end fund? The answer is the number of shares outstanding. An open-end mutual fund issues shares to the public based on, primarily, the publics willingness and desire to purchase its shares. In other words, the fund generally has no limit on the number of shares it issues. For example, if the fund has issued 1 million shares and the public continued to purchase more shares, the fund would simply continue to issue shares to meet public demand. The open-end fund could have 1, 2, or 10 million shares outstanding at any given point in time. Ah,...you're starting to get it!!! The amount of shares are dynamic, always changing. The outstanding shares are unspecified, unset, and ..."**open**." Hence the term, open end fund. One final point, open end funds do not trade on any exchange, but rather are bought from and redeemed by the management company. These securities trade according to their Net Asset Value (NAV).

Closed End Fund
Now, what might you suspect is the distinguishing characteristic of "closed end funds?" With closed-end funds, outstanding shares are fixed. Closed ends (generally) make a one time issuance of stock. These securities are neither bought from nor redeemed by the management company, but rather are traded on exchanges in the same manner as common stock. An investor wishing to purchase shares in a closed-end fund must enter into the marketplace and buy shares from other shareholders. These securities trade according to prices set in the marketplace.

Now that we understand the two different types of mutual funds, let's review the general characteristics found in all mutual funds.

Fund Sponsor
Each mutual fund must have a fund sponsor. That sponsor has the responsibility for bringing the fund "public." The fund sponsor may be a general underwriting firm such as Merrill Lynch, or a company specializing in mutual funds such as Fidelity and Charles Schwab. Each fund must be registered with the Securities and Exchange Commission.

Prospectus
A useful (at least for me) word association to instill the meaning of prospectus in your mind, it to think of someone prospecting for gold. That is exactly what the prospectus is attempting to do. It is the document which states all the salient or important information about that particular fund. Enclosed within the prospectus will be information on the sales charges or lack thereof, the managers, the investment objective, the various expenses, the funds' largest holdings, etc, (you get the picture).

This document is essentially prospecting for new gold, new money. This is the one document which is absolutely essential to understanding the specifics of any mutual fund.

Investment Advisor

All mutual funds will have an investment advisor. This is the individual, specified in the prospectus, who will be responsible for the funds' investment decisions.

Management Fee

Management fees, are common to all mutual funds. However, there can be a vast difference in the amount of these charges, impacting greatly the total return of the fund over time. Therefore, they should be closely watched and compared with other suitable funds.

Custodian Bank

All funds have a "custodian bank." The bank's duties include the safeguarding of assets, performing the role of transfer agent, and acting as the general record keeper for the fund.

Mutual funds can be structured as diversified or non-diversified. The differences are outlined below:

Diversified Funds

A diversified fund has three primary rules to which it adheres:

1) 75 % or more of its assets invested in securities;
2) No more than 5% of its assets invested in any one issuer;
3) A maximum holding of 10% of the voting securities in any one issuer.

Most all mutual funds are diversified funds. In fact, the diversification element of mutual funds, is one of the most highly regarded of all mutual fund benefits.

Non-Diversified Fund

Finally, any fund which does not adhere to the above specified criteria is categorized as a "non-diversified" fund. While these funds are very limited in number, they do exist. Whether the fund is diversified or non-diversified is stated in the prospectus.

Purpose and Benefits of Mutual Funds

Ability to Invest

Imagine you were an individual with relatively small savings, and a very modest income. Where could you invest your money? Well, you could try stocks or bonds–but with a small amount of money with which to begin and an even smaller amount to invest on a future regular basis, the commissions you would incur would consume a substantial portion of the funds available for investment. In short, there was a need for some investment vehicle that would allow small investors access to the same investment choices available to larger investors.

Professional Management

Larger investors have also enjoyed the luxury of having an experienced financial consultant(s) assist in the development and implementation of their investment strategies. Small investors, again, were not afforded such assistance. Where there is a genuine need, usually an entrepreneur will find a genuine solution. The "Mutual Fund" filled this long unsatisfied need.

Diversification

Last, we have the benefit of diversification. It is an acknowledged rule of nature that diversification is a prudent human behavior. This rule supersedes financial investment, and indeed permeates all of society. An example would be the saying, "Don't put all of your eggs in the same basket." (I would imagine the person who coined that phrase, learned the hard way.) The principle applies to a basket of eggs or a basket of financial securities. At any time, some event could occur causing a particular stock to decline precipitously in value. If you happen to be invested in that stock, I think you get the picture. However, the odds are considerably smaller that some event would cause all of your stocks to suffer a similar fate. Herein lies the long standing acknowledged benefits of diversification.

Hooray for Mutual Funds

Eventually financial people (advisors, planner, and manager) started to realize that there was a vast pool of financial assets in American households not invested, and set out to address the barriers that were precluding the masses from the financial markets. What do you think their solution was? You guessed it, "mutual funds."

It truly was a **hooray** for mutual funds. With the introduction of mutual funds, the publics participation in the financial markets, has increased beyond what anyone thought possible just 20 years ago. Mutual funds have, in fact, not only revolutionized a new method of investing, but have also, for the first time in history, put the individual investor on much the same level as the large institutional investor.

Now that we understand the basics of mutual funds, and why they came into existence, let's look at the different types of mutual funds.

Types of Mutual Funds

There are many different types of mutual funds. For our purposes, we will focus on the most well known, standard types.

Growth Fund   The growth fund, is a fund which seeks to invest the fund's capital in vehicles which will yield higher rates of "**growth**" over the long term. Its primary objective is long-term appreciation of capital. Generally, younger people are more **heavily** invested in growth funds.

Income Fund   The income fund seeks to invest in securities which will yield higher flows of "**income**" to its shareholders. For instance, this type of fund would be more heavily invested in preferred stocks, utilities, and fixed income securities, all of which traditionally yield higher income streams. The typical investor would be somewhat older and more financially secure.

Growth and Income   Again, as it name would imply, this type of fund seeks to provide its investors with growth and income. Not much more to say about this one.

Balanced Fund   The balanced fund seeks to provide its investors with modest gains and income in a bull market, and less downside or risk in a bear market. The primary objective is to preserve original investment capital while providing some capital gain. Again, this fund type would typically attract more established investors.

Specialized Fund   This type of fund "specializes" in a particular industry or geographic region. For example, gold funds, technology funds, or international funds would all be examples of specialized funds.

Special Situation Fund   These funds invest in special situations such as companies in bankruptcy or takeover candidates.

Hedge Fund   Hedge funds are relatively new to the mutual fund game, and invest in virtually all (stocks, bonds, futures, and currencies) financial securities.

Trading of Open and Closed End Funds

Open End Open end fund shares are continuously issued by the fund sponsor. When an investor wishes to buy, new shares are issued, no one else is "required" to sell. If an investor wishes to sell, the issuer buys or "redeems" the shares. No other investor is actually buying those shares. Open end shares cannot be bought and sold between individuals. They can only be purchased or redeemed through the issuing company.

Net Asset Value (NAV) The net asset value is computed on a daily basis. It is this value at which shares are bought and sold. This value represents the value of all securities held by the fund, divided by the total number of shares outstanding. The NAV fluctuates based upon the changing prices of securities in the portfolio.

No-Load If the fund is a "no-load," shares can be purchased at the NAV price. If the fund has sales or load charges, the purchaser must add this fee to the NAV price to arrive at the total purchase price. Recently, no-load funds have become very popular with the investing public, and increased exponentially with respect to the number of funds and assets under management.

Money Market Money markets are also a type of open-end mutual fund, with one notable distinction: as the fund produces earnings, the investor realizes more "shares" instead of more "dollars" per share. In other words, their price is fixed at $1.00. This is because they are considered to be a temporary holding place for funds waiting to be invested.

For example, if an investor has $1,000 in a money market, that investor will have 1000 shares. If the funds are invested for the full year and returns 5%, the investor would normally have 1,000 shares worth $1.05 per share. Not so with money markets. This extra $50 dollars is automatically reinvested into more fund shares because the share price does not fluctuate. One final note on money market funds. While share prices do not fluctuate, or I should say have not fluctuated, there is no law preventing this from occurring. One day share prices might fluctuate,...up or DOWN!!!

Forward Pricing

Mutual funds are purchased under what is called "forward pricing." This term refers to the fact that the mutual fund investor purchases securities at a price to be specified in the **future**. Why? If you recall from our discussion on net asset value (NAV), this price is calculated after the close of business for that trading day. Therefore, when an investor places an order at 2:30 p.m. to buy $5,000 of AAA mutual fund, the broker cannot quote a purchase price because the holdings of the fund are still actively trading. Only after the close, can the closing prices be obtained and the NAV calculated. It is this NAV closing price at which the investor is purchasing the shares.

Redemption Fee

Some mutual funds impose fees on investors who sell or redeem their shares, usually if done so before a specified time period. The mutual fund company does not want its investors for the short term, but rather for the long term. Therefore, if the investment is not held for a certain period of time, "**redemption fees**" may apply.

Reinvestment of Dividends

Mutual funds pay two types of dividends: regular dividends and capital gains dividends. The investor has the option of having one or both dividend types reinvested automatically. If this option is elected, the dividends will be reinvested at NAV, without any sales charges. The investor, also has the option to elect cash disbursement of dividends.

Fund Family Switching

Certain mutual funds are lumped together in what is termed "**fund families**." Within these fund families, investors are allowed to "switch," or sell one fund and reinvest the proceeds to another fund in the same family. These same family switches, are allowed generally commission free and sales charge free. An example of fund families would be Scudder Funds, Templeton Funds, and American Funds. Many brokerage firms are now allowing customers to "switch" between any of there mutual funds commission free. This practice, has been pioneered by Charles Schwab & Co. Inc. Schwab currently has more than 500 "no-load" mutual funds in their "Mutual Fund Marketplace," wherein investors can switch between any fund or fund family commission free.

Closed End Trading

Closed

A closed-end fund is a publicly traded management company. The fund is capitalized by a one-time issuance of stock. After that issuance, the funds books are "closed." No new shares will be issued. Subsequent to the public issuance of securities, the fund trades on an exchange just like a stock.

It is important to recognize that closed-end funds do not trade according to net asset value. Closed end funds trade according to an arbitrary value assigned by the investing public. For example, if there were a sudden rumor that gold reserves were dangerously low, gold related securities might trade appreciably higher, even if gold prices had not risen very much. Therefore, if you compared two mutual funds which were exclusively invested in "actual" gold reserves, the open-end fund, priced according to NAV, would still trade at approximately the same price; whereas the closed-end fund, only pegged to public sentiment and demand, would probably exhibit a marked increase in its per share price.

Because of this phenomenon, closed in funds can trade at, above, or below net asset value. When they are trading "above" NAV, they are said to be trading at a premium. When trading below, they are trading at a "discount." (By now these terms should sound familiar, if not you might want to review chapter two on Debt Securities) The financial pages will usually list closed end funds by name, exchange, NAV, public price, and % difference. An example is shown below:

Close End Fund	Exch.	NAV	Price	% Diff.
ABC Fund	NYSE	8.60	9.43	+.09
123 Fund	AMEX	7.20	7.28	+.01
Her Fund	NYSE	10.10	9.58	-.05

Not Redeemable   One last point on trading of closed-end funds. When an investor wishes to liquidate the holding, the fund shares are **not** redeemed to the fund issuer. Rather they are sold on an exchange to another investor at the prevailing marketing price.

Mutual Fund Income and Expenses

As I mentioned earlier, mutual funds are a type of company, specifically, a management investment company. As such, they also have income statements. They are not as involved and complex as those of regular corporations, but rather they have only two primary categories; investment income and operational related expenses. A sample income statement is listed below.

Mutual Fund Income Statement

Investment Income		$50,000,000

Expenses:

Management Fee:	$5,000,000
Brokerage Fees:	$2,000,000
Custodial Fees:	$ 500,000
Printing Fees:	$ 400,000
Legal & Audit:	$1,000,000
Administrative:	$ 500,000

Total Expenses	$9,400,000

Net Investment Income	$40,600,000

Let's assume that the above referenced mutual fund has $500,000,000 in net assets invested. The $50,000,000 investment income represents a somewhat typical 10% return. The above listed expenses are briefly detailed below.

Management Fee

This is the fee charged by the fund managers for the services they provide. This fee is usually the largest expense of the fund, and typically runs between one-half and two percent of assets under management.

Brokerage Fees

Brokerage fees are a significant fee. Most funds do not utilize the services of "discount" brokerage firms, causing this expense item to be higher than necessary.

Custodial Fees

This is the fee paid to the bank which acts as the primary record keeper. This bank is also responsible for the safekeeping of the fund's monetary assets and the disbursements of those funds to investors.

Printing Fees   Can you think of any printing the mutual fund mght require?   Of course, chief among all would be the prospectus. Others might include advertising and sales literature.

Legal & Audit   In order to establish a fund, it must be registered with the Securities and Exchange Commission (SEC).   This registration process involves the filing of very legally complex documents usually prepared by securities attorneys. Also, mutual funds are required to have at least an annual audit.   Most funds conduct semi-annual as well as annual audits.

Administrative Fee   Fairly self explanatory, this expense is associated with office staff and other non-management personnel.

Expenses Ratio   Mutual Funds, as with other corporations, have some managers that are better at "running the corporation" than others.   I am not referring to the investment advisors, but rather managers whose primary responsibility is to "manage" the fund efficiently.   In order to gauge and thus compare this efficiency, a ratio termed the "**expense ratio**" is used.   The formula is presented below:

$$\text{Expense Ratio} = \frac{\text{Total Expenses}}{\text{Total Net Assets}} = \frac{\$9,400,000}{\$500,000,000} = 1.9\%$$

This ratio tells the investor what percent must be subtracted from the total return to get net or real return.   The expense ratio should be used to assist in the selection process. The lower the ratio, the more efficient the operation of the fund; the higher the ratio, the less efficient.

Review and Comparison of Open-End and Closed-End Mutual Funds

	Open End	**Closed End**
1) Number of shares outstanding	Contantly Changing	Fixed
2) Public Offering	Continuous	One Time
3) Redemption By Issuer	Yes	No
4) Selling Price	Net Asset Value	Set By Market
5) Where shares are bought or sold	Can be bought from an issuer or underwriter although most commonly purchased from a dealer.	On an Exchange, or Over-the-Counter.
6) From whom shares are purchased, or to whom shares are sold.	Purchased from and sold to an underwriter through a securities broker	Purchased and sold to investors in marketplace.
7) Relation of purchase price to Net Asset Value	Purchase Price is net asset value plus commission or sales charge.	No relation to asset value. Purchase price is determined by supply and demand in the marketplace.
8) Buying or selling cost or charges	A sales charge is added to NAV to arrive at the purchase price. If a no-load, no charges are added.	Since these trade like stocks, there is commission charged for both purchases and sales.

Exchange Traded Funds ETF's

Exchange Traded Funds, or ETf's are index funds which trade just like stocks on major stock exchanges. For investors wanting to invest in various segements of the market quickly and cheaply, ETF's are the most pratical manner. ETF's also allow investors access to markets that were out of reach to average investors just a few short years ago. For example, individual investors now have the ability to invest in commodities markets such as gold, silver, and oil, through their regular stock brokerage account by utilizing ETF's.

While ETF's are technically mutual funds, they trade just like stock, very similar to closed end funds. ETF's have opened entirely new horizons for investors and have exploded in popularity over the years. The American Stock Exchange has been a pioneer in this new investment arena and provides a wealth of information related to ETF's on their website, www.amex.com.

BreakPoints

Mutual Funds which have sales charges, often offer discounts on those sales charges at certain points of asset ownership. The amount of an asset the investor must own in order to receive the sales charge discount varies from fund to fund, and the investor should check the prospectus or inquire to the brokerage firm to confirm the levels.

Often, the levels need not be reached in one account, or in one purchase. Many mutual funds allow for these sales charge discounts if members of the same family, in aggregate, meet the required asset levels. In addition, if an investors intends to purchase enough of a fund to meet the required levels in future purchases, then the discounts may also be applied to the current purchase. Just remember, if you intend to purchase mutual funds with sales charges, always ask about breakpoint discounts.

5

Securities Markets

"...What we think or what we
   believe is, in the end, of little
   consequence. The only thing
   of consequence is what we do..."

John Ruskin
(1819-1900)
English art critic and historian

SECURITIES MARKETS

Negotiable securities trade in specific "markets." The overall market-place for securities is divided into two types of markets:

1) Primary Market
2) Secondary Market

Primary Market   The term primary market refers to the marketplace where "new issues" or initial public offerings are traded.

Secondary Market   Conversely, the term secondary market refers to the marketplace where existing securities are traded.

The overwhelming majority of trading takes place in the secondary market. Therefore, it is this market which will be the focus of our discussion. It is important to understand the divisions or classifications within the secondary market. They are:

1) First Market
2) Second Market
3) Third Market
4) Fourth Market

First Market   The first market is trading of exchange listed securities on the floor of the stock exchange. This was the first market, as the New York Stock Exchange (NYSE) is about 200 years old. The NYSE is the largest stock exchange by far, followed by the American Stock Exchange (AMEX). These exchanges have very specific requirements that companies must meet in order to have thier stock listed. Both of these exchanges, among other things, require that companies have a **national** investor base. As of this writing, daily volume on the NYSE averages over a billion shares per day.

The American Stock Exchange is much smaller than the NYSE, and generally list companies that do not meet NYSE listing requirements. Over the years, the American Stock Exchange has changed and is now considered predominant exchange fot trading ETF's.

Regional Exchanges

There are also regional exchanges which trade companies specific to that region, and they may also trade some NYSE and AMEX listed issues (called "dual listings"). These regional exchanges are:

1) Midwest (Chicago)
2) Pacific (Los Angeles)
3) Philadelphia
4) Boston
5) Cincinnati

Dual Listing

The regional stock exchanges are much smaller than the NYSE. It is very important to understand that dual listings do not occur between the NYSE, AMEX, and NASDAQ. These marketplaces are very competitive with one another and always require exclusive listing agreements. Thus, a NYSE listed security will never be listed on the NASDAQ or AMEX simultaneously, and vice versa. However, these three dominant markets do not consider the regional exchanges a "threat" and will therefore permit dual listings there.

Second Market

The second market is trading of securities which are not traded on any exchange,...they are traded "Over-The-Counter" (OTC). The second market developed itself in the 1900s with the invention of the telephone. Instead of needing a place to meet and trade (exchange floor), trading could now take place over the phone. The OTC market trades a greater number of companies than the listed exchanges, and recently volume has started to rival and at times exceed the listed exchange volume.

It is regulated by the National Association of Securities Dealers (NASD). Well over 10,000 companies trade OTC, with trading concentrated in about 5,000 issues. OTC companies that meet certain requirements are quoted on the NASDAQ (NASD Automated Quotation) system.

The NASD's requirements for listing on NASDAQ are less stringent than the NYSE, and most startups begin trading OTC. As a company grows and matures, it may move its listing to the NYSE or AMEX, or it may elect to stay in the NASDAQ market.

Third Market The third market is trading of exchange listed securities which takes place "off the floor." The third market developed in the 1960s. The NYSE has a rule which states, parenthetically, that a member firm, during hours when the exchange is open, must execute the trade on the exchange floor. However, non-member firms are not subject to this rule.

The third market did not really begin to flourish until the 1980's, during which time, a global market developed in NYSE traded issues. The most significant feature of third market makers is that they stay open 24 hours! That's right, an investor can buy or sell stocks through these brokers all day and all night. Of course, that doesn't necessarily mean that you will be receiving the best price on your buy or sell transactions. In response to the third market, the NYSE enacted in 1991 an "after hours" trading session conducted after the normal 4:00pm close. This is just the beginning, eventually the NYSE, it is thought, will also move to 24 hours trading. (We will see.)

Fourth Market   The fourth market is a direct market which consist of institutional investors who trade "directly" with one another. This market developed in the 1960's as a way to circumvent the NYSE's fixed commission rates. Under the NYSE fixed commission rate structure, large institutional orders did not get any type of discount which resulted in a much higher "cost" of trading. To eliviate this problem, firms decided to trade directly with one another at much lower commission rates. It is very important to note, that this trading behavior, eventually caused the entire stock commission structure to be deregulated; giving birth to a totally new segment in the stock brokerage industry which we know today as "Discount Stock Brokers."

Instinet   Instinet (Institutional Network) was the vehicle developed to facilitate this "trading" between institutional investors. After the 1975 deregulation of commissions, NYSE brokers began giving large discounts to institutions, thereby eliminating to a certain degree, the need for instinet. In 1991 instinet was purchase by REUTERS and subsequently repositioned to serve as a global electronic trading system rather than an institutional only trading system. Thus far, the strategy has proven to be a very successful one.

Because most of the volume, and even more so for the individual investor, takes place on the first and second markets, this is where we will focus our discussion.

The first market deals with the Stock Exchange. Exactly what is a stock exchange?

Stock Exchange   A stock exchange is a private association of individuals (brokers), with the main purpose of providing a central meeting place for its members to trade securities. This central meeting place is called the "Floor or Trading Floor".

It is important to remember that a stock exchange itself does not own any of the securities traded on its floor. Nor does the stock exchange itself buy or sell any of the securities traded on the exchange. Rather, the securities are owned by the member firm's customers or by the member firms themselves.

It is also important to remember that a stock exchange does not establish or fix the price at which any security is traded. The price is determined by a free and open **"auction"** type of trading. The price depends on the demand and supply relationship of that security at a particular time. In other words, if there are more seller of a stock than buyers, the price of the stock will tend to go lower. If there are more buyers of a stock than sellers, then the price of the stock will tend to trade higher. **Remember the price of any security is determined by supply and demand**.

Now let us turn our focus to the stock exchanges themselves.

In order to be listed on the NYSE, a company has to meet several minimum requirements; the company must have:

- 2000 shareholders owning at least 100 common shares

- 100,000 shares average monthly trading volume for the last 6 months

- 1,100,000 publicly held shares

- $18,000,000 aggregate market value of publicly held shares

- $2,500,000 of earnings before tax for the last fiscal year

In addition to the numerical requirements, the NYSE has several non-numerical standards. They are:

1) Evidence of national public interest in trading the shares

2) Evidence that share ownership is spread nationally

3) Evidence that the company is a growing concern with good prospects

The NYSE is usually reluctant to delist stocks, but will consider delisting if:

- The number of shareholders with 100 shares or more falls below 1200

- Number of publicly held shares falls below 600,000

- Aggregate market value of stock falls below $5,000,000

- The company substantially reduces the scope of its operations

- The company files for bankruptcy

- The company issues a class of non-voting stock

- The company fails to solicit proxies for annual meetings

The NYSE can also delist a company for a variety of other reasons, such as the failure to keep good accounting practices, inability to meet debt obligations, failure to make adequate disclosure to the public, and others.

Suffice it to say that the NYSE can delist a company for any material reason, if it believes the delisting is in the best interest of the exchange and/or the public. Now let us examine the listing requirements of the American Stock Exchange. (AMEX)

The AMEX's requirements are much less stringent. They are: *

- 1200 shareholders owning at least 100 shares , of which 500 must own between 100 and 500 shares

- 400,000 shares held by the general public

- $750,000 of earnings before tax for the last fiscal year

- $300,000 of aggregate value of shares held by public

* **Note**: These requirements are dynamic and thus have a tendency to change over time.

As with the NYSE, the AMEX can delist a company if it no longer meets its numerical criteria and if there is a material reason which the exchange feels delisting would be in the best interest of the exchange and/or the public.

How The Exchange Functions

Auction Market

As mentioned earlier, the NYSE is an auction market. Orders for exchange-listed stocks are sent via wire to booths on the side of the exchange floor. There the order is written on a ticket and given to a floor trader who takes the order to the trading post on the exchange floor where that stock trades.

Floor Trader

Floor traders are employees of each brokerage firm. If the floor traders are very busy, the firm can have a $2 broker perform the trade. $2 brokers are independent traders who assist brokerage firms, helping them execute trades. The name stems from the fact that they used to be paid $2 per trade. Also on the floor of the exchange

Competitive Trader

are competitive traders, who trade only for their own accounts.

The Specialist

Trading Post

Specialist trade one or more specific stocks at their particular trading post on the exchange floor. Their activity is vital to the maintenance of a free and continuous market in the specific issues they represent. They are responsible for conducting the auction at the post.

Auction

If you have ever been to an auction, you are familiar with the auctioneer referring to the item for sale an

Bids

receiving "**bids**" for the item. This type of auction is called a one way auction. Now assume for a moment, that there were other auctioneers at this same auction, and while buyers were bidding 10, 10.25, or 10.50, some

Offers

of these other auctioneers were "offering" to sell their item (the same item) at 11, 10.75, or 10.50. In this event, you would have a two way auction. Buyers would be giving their "bids", the price at which they are willing to buy, and sellers would be making their "offers," the price at which they are willing to sell. When a buyers bid and a sellers offer matched one another, a transaction would take place. This is exactly how the buying and selling activity takes place on the NYSE. It is a two way auction market.

At The Market The above illustrated auction example is how limit orders are executed on the listed exchanges. However, what happens when an order to buy or sell "**at the market**" is received? An order to buy or sell at the market is basically an order to buy or sell "**right now**." Therefore, the order is taken immediately to the specialist post and the specialist will give the customer the best bid (for sellers) or offer (for buyers) available at that specific time.

Dealer and Broker A specialist functions in a dual capacity as a dealer and as a broker. As a dealer, the specialist buys or sells for his own account to maintain a fair and orderly market in the stocks in which he specializes. As a broker, the specialist will "pass off" orders to other brokers.

Commission Markup When the specialist functions as a dealer, he charges the customer a mark-up. When the specialist functions as a broker, surprise-surprise, he charges a commission.

Specialist Book The specialist book is where limit orders are entered for him to track and monitor. The book is a loose leaf notebook with space for buy orders on the left, and sell orders on the right. There is a book for each stock in which the specialist trades. The orders are entered in the book by the specialist according to price and in the sequence in which they are received by him at the post. He notes the number of shares, the name of the firm placing the order, and whether the order is "good-till-cancelled" (GTC). When orders are executed by a specialist, they are executed in the same sequence in which the orders were recorded in his book at that particular price.

The specialist book gives rise to the familiar term frequently used with limit orders, that is "**stock ahead**." Suppose you have an order to sell IBM at 95 1/4, the next day you check the newspaper and find that IBM traded as high as 95 1/4, you would probably assume that your order had been executed. Upon receiving no notification from your broker, you phone him/her and find that your order did not execute. The question is ....Why? Well, remember that orders are placed on the specialist book in sequence with which they are received. So, if your order was to sell 1000 shares at 95 1/4, and there was another order to sell 1000 shares of IBM which was placed prior to your order with the same price, then that order - naturally, would be ahead of your order and executed first. Now with this particular example, further assume that the buyer for IBM at 95 1/4 only wanted 1000 shares. The specialist would fill the order that is first in line, and your order would move up on the specialist book to the top spot. When you call your broker, you will ask why your order was not filled, and your broker would accurately respond, "stock ahead."

Super Dot Today, most trades are transmitted to the specialist post by a communication system known as the **Designated Order Turnaround** (**DOT**) system, also termed "Super DOT." The DOT system delivers orders directly to a specialist clerk who hands the order to the specialist. The specialist then decides how best to handle or fill the order.

In this system there is no auction in the usual sense. However, the system does allow the specialist to handle a much larger volume in a much more efficient manner.

THE OVER-THE-COUNTER MARKET

Securities are bought and sold in two general types of markets: the stock exchanges, which deal in securities of companies which have applied and qualified for exchange trading (listed securities), and the "Over-The-Counter" market, which handles all other securities transactions. Any transaction that does not take place on the floor of an exchange, takes place over-the-counter.

Negotiated

The **Over-The-Counter** market is a national "**negotiated**" market, without a central market place, without a trading floor, composed of a computer network of thousands of brokers and dealers transacting securities trades for themselves and their customers. Professional buyers and sellers seek each other out electronically and by telephone and negotiate prices on the most favorable basis that can be achieved. Often these negotiations are accomplished in seconds, also there is no auction procedure comparable to that on the floor of a exchange.

Market Marker

The most important person on the stock exchange is the specialist. His equal, in the over-the-counter market, is the "market maker." The market maker, is an individual or company whom is registered, licensed, and holds an inventory in one or more stocks. The market maker sells stocks from his inventory to customers, and buys stock for his inventory from customers. At the end of the day, the market maker is holding stocks in inventory; meaning the market maker has assumed the risk for his inventory.

Risk Assumption

For example, suppose the market maker is currently holding 100,000 shares of Intel, 200,000 shares of IBM, 50,000 shares of Microsoft, and 150,000 shares of Cisco Systems. If these stocks should fall while the market maker holds them in inventory, obviously he would suffer substantial losses. Conversely, if these securities should rise significantly while in inventory, the market maker would reap huge profits. Herein lies the salient point of market makers, not only do they deal with the public and provide essential liquidity to the market, they also **assume risk** for their own account or inventory.

OTC Issues
All new issues are initially sold OTC. After issuance, the securities are either listed on an exchange or traded over-the-counter. Open ended mutual funds and limited partnership are also sold initially OTC, but most of these do not trade. Open ended mutual funds are redeemed by the issuer, and most limited partnerships are normally non-negotiable and held until the program is terminated.

NASD
National Association of Securities Dealers (NASD) is the regulatory body which oversees the OTC market. The NASD will be covered in more detail in the chapter dealing with Self Regulatory Organizations. (SRO's)

Pink Sheets
Well over 10,000 stocks trade on the OTC market. These securities are quoted on pink sheets of paper aptly named the "**pink sheets.**" Pink sheets are published daily and are sold to dealers on a subscription basis.

NASDAQ
Of the approximately 10,000 stocks trading on the OTC market, about 5,000 are large enough to be included on the NASD Automated Quotations System. (NASDAQ) The NASDAQ system allows OTC market makers to display bids and offers electronically (rather than on Pink Sheets) for eligible stocks, so that interested members can call each other and trade.

Bulletin Board
"Bulletin Board" quotes are the latest addition to the OTC quote systems. As you probably surmised, quoting stocks once a day on paper, with all subsequent quotes

having to occur by telephone, could be quite cumbersome and time consuming. The solution, an electronically linked quote system without the requirements of the NASDAQ system. The quotes on this system are called "**bulletin board**" quotes. As you might have already guessed, the bulletin board quote system has rendered the pink sheets virtually useless and obsolete.

NASDAQ NMS
The NASDAQ system only gave bid and ask quotes - it did not show actual trades as they occurred as the NYSE does. Therefore, the NASDAQ **National Market System** was developed to provide the same detailed trade information as was available on the NYSE; namely the ability to show actual trades as they occur. Thus, there is a running tape of NASDAQ NMS stock trading as it occurs.

PARAMETERS OF ACCEPTABLE ORDERS

Although there are several exchanges and two primary markets, the good news is that practically all use the same types of order qualifications. These qualifications are listed and explained below.

Types of Orders

There are basically four types of orders:

- Market Order
- Limit Order
- Stop Order
- Stop Limit Order

Market Order
A market order is an order to be executed immediately, that is, to be executed at the best possible price as soon as it reaches the **executing broker**. Market orders are

the most common of all orders. The greatest advantage of the market order is speed. The customer specifies no price in this type of order, he or she merely instructs the broker to buy or sell at the best available price. Because the investor specifies no price, but only ask that the order be executed at the best possible price, **market orders will always be executed**. Remember, in a market order, you are literally saying, "I will **pay** whatever it takes to buy this stock", or "I will **accept** whatever you offer me to sell this stock".

Limit Order The primary characteristic of the limit order is that the customer decides **in advance** on the **price** at which he or she is willing to trade. The customer believes that their price is one that will be reached and is willing to wait until that happens, even at the risk of the order **not being executed** in the near or distant future.

Or Better In the execution of a limit order, the broker is to execute the order at the limit price "**or better**." **Better** means that a limit order to buy is executed at the customers price or lower. Conversely, a sell limit order is executed at the customers price or higher. If the broker can obtain a "better" price for the customer than the one specified, he or she is obligated to do so. Every limit order is automatically given the status "**or better**."

Stop Order A "stop order" is an order designed to execute a trade at a specified price. A stop order is placed below the current market price if you are selling, and above the current price if you are buying. The stop order is also referred to as a stop loss order. Why? Assume IBM is bid 95 and ask 95 1/8. Further assume that you purchased IBM at 91. You feel IBM may go higher, but you also do not want to risk all of the profit you have already gained. You're willing to allow the stock to drop to 94, but no lower. So, what do you do? You might elect to place a stop or stop loss order (these are one in the same). You would simply call your broker and instruct him or her to place a stop loss order at 94. What you have just instructed him or her to do, is to place an order which will enable you to hold IBM as long as it continues higher. However, if IBM should start to drop, you will sell if it falls to 94. When and if IBM falls to 94, your stop loss order will automatically turn into a market order and will be executed at best possible price. What we have just described is an example of a "sell stop" loss order.

Sell Stop

There is also, as you might have guessed, an order termed a "buy" stop order. You would place this order when you wanted to buy a stock at a price higher than its current price. Why would you want to do this? Basically for technical reasons. If you use technical research to aid you in deciding when to buy, at times this research would indicate a buy of a particular stock only at a specific price. And yes, sometimes that buy price is above the current price. Normally, if you were to place an order above the current price, you would be executed at the current price. The specialist or market maker are prohibited from filling away from the current market price. Therefore, if the stock is bid 95 and offered at 95 1/4, you could not place an order to buy at 96 without special instructions to the executing broker. The special instruction necessary is the "**buy stop**" qualifier added to the order. With this qualifier, you are instructing the executing broker to buy the stock for you only if the stock reaches 96. Again, if you placed an order to buy at 96 while the stock was currently offered at 95 1/4 without this qualifier, your broker would, and rightfully so, execute your order at 95 1/4.

Buy Stop

Stop Limit Order

The stop limit order works exactly the same as the stop order with one very important distinguishing factor. That is, your order will **ONLY** be executed at the stop limit price. If you recall from our stop order section, once the stock trades at or below your specified stop price, your order automatically turns into a **market** order. However, with a stop **limit order**, your order becomes a regular limit order once the stock trades **at or below** your specified stop limit price. To illustrate this difference more clearly, let us look at an example.

Let's suppose that Sears is bid 45 and ask 45 1/8. You purchased the stock 1 year ago at 36. You currently have 9 points of profit and wish to protect at least some of this profit. You therefore decide to place a stop order. Should you place a stop order or a stop limit order? Lets look at both scenarios.

First the stop order. You place your stop order at 42. Now assume the stock start to fall, and over the next week or two the stock finally trades at 42, your stop price. Accordingly, your stop order would turn into a market order and you would be executed at the next **"available"** price. The term "available" is a key term because your order, now a market order, may or may not be executed at 42. Frequently, the order is executed at an 1/8 and sometimes even a 1/4 below the stop price. The reason is because market orders are executed at the best available price when received by specialist or market maker. Therefore, if the stock is falling quickly, your order may be filled a tick or two below the original stop price. There is another possible risk one encounters when placing stop orders. Assume there is some bad news which comes out during the hours when the market is closed. Well, when Sears opens the next trading day, shockingly the stock opens at 32. Where will your order be executed? You guessed it, at or around 32. It is critically important to remember, a stop order becomes a market order when the stock trades **at or below** your specified stop price. In the above example, the stock opening at 32 is **below** your your stop price of 42, and therefore your stop order becomes a market order and is executed accordingly.

Stop Limit Order Cont.

Second the stop limit order. Again, lets use the same example. Sears stock is bid 45 and ask 45 1/8, however, in this scenario you set a stop limit order at 42 instead of a stop order.

Well, again presume over the next few weeks the stock falls until it reaches 42. At this point, your order **does not** become a market order, but rather remains a limit order. With an orderly decline in price as indicated in this example, your stop limit order will probably be executed at your **stop limit** price of 42. If the market maker or specialist is unable to execute the order at 42, then the order remains in effect at that price.

Now let's look at the second scenario. Bad news is released during the hours the market is closed, and the stock opens at 32. What happens to your stop limit order? Nothing!! Your stop limit order does not turn into a market order and therefore does not execute and remains in effect.

The salient point - a **stop limit** order can only be executed at your stop limit price. Conversely, a **stop order** (or stop loss order) turns into a market order once the stock trades at or below your stop price, and is therefore subject to executions very far away from your original stop price.

As shown from the previous example, there are times when stop orders are more appropriate, and times when stop limits are more appropriate. It is the investor's responsibility to ascertain which order should be used in a given situation, and to be cognizant of the risks associated with each.

ORDER QUALIFIERS

When placing any order, buy or sell, there are certain instructions the investor is allowed to give the executing broker. These instructions are referred to in the brokerage industry as "**qualifiers**." While most qualifiers are accepted at all brokerage firms, there may be a few which are not accepted by your particular firm. To prevent any surprises at the time of order placement, it would be wise to check with your brokerage firm to clarify which qualifiers they do or do not accept. Below, we will list and briefly explain the most common of these qualifiers.

Good Till Cancelled (GTC)   Perhaps the most well known of all the qualifiers is the GTC or Good Till Cancelled qualifier. This qualifier is quite simply what it says. Basically, when a GTC is used with an order, it instructs the executing broker to leave the order "**open**" in the order file until it is either executed or cancelled by the investor. Some firms have time limits on the duration of GTC orders, and some do not. Again, you should check with your particular brokerage firm to clarify their GTC rules.

All Or None (AON)   An AON or "all or none" qualifier also is quite straightforward. With an AON attached to an order, the investor is instructing the broker to execute the entire order or none of the order. The client is stating unequivocally that he does not want a partial execution. The result of this qualifier may or may not be desirable, it just depends on ones perspective, goals and objectives.

Fill Or Kill (FOK)

A FOK or "fill or kill" qualifier instructs the broker to attempt to execute the order immediately, but to only do so once. If the broker is unable to execute the order on the **first** try, then the broker must cancel the order. The broker cannot attempt to "shop" the order and try to execute it again later. The order must be "filled" or "killed" immediately. Most firms offer FOK qualifier, but as previously stated some may not.

Immediate Or Cancel (IOC)

This qualifier is very similar to the fill or kill qualifier with one notable exception; the order can be filled either in part of in full. This qualifier says the order must be executed immediately, and if it is only partially filled, the remaining portion of the order must be cancelled. There can be no attempts, other than the first try, to execute the order.

Not Held

A "not held" qualifier is generally used in tandem with market orders. Generally, a market order is to be filled immediately at the best prevailing price. However, there are times when a broker, particularly floor brokers, might have a better idea of whether the price of your stock is about to rise, fall, or stay the same. If you submit your order with a not held qualifier attached, you are giving your broker permission to execute your order at what he or she thinks is the best available time and price. The risk, of course, is that your broker could execute your order at a time and price that is not to your satisfaction. If this occurs, you have no recourse, because you have given your permission for this type of execution. Obviously, this qualifier should be used with extreme caution.

Discretionary

Discretionary is not really a qualifier but more so a type of account, although it can be used as a qualifier on certain orders; therefore we will cover it in this section.

Basically, this type of qualifier or account gives the broker the authorization, usually through a power of attorney, to select not only the time and price of executions but also what security is purchased or sold. In other words, the broker has complete "discretion" over **what** to buy or sell, and **when** to buy or sell. If the client is dissatisfied with the brokers buy and sell decisions, the only recourse is to terminate the agreement with respect to future trades.

Do Not Reduce (DNR) As we have already established in a previous chapter, when cash dividends are paid, the outstanding orders for the stock are reduced by the amount of the dividend. Use of the DNR qualifier instructs your broker not to reduce your order if a dividend should be paid prior to the execution of your order. Regardless of any dividend paid, your order will remain at its original price.

At the Open "At the opening" is a qualifier which instructs your broker to execute your order at the opening price or cancel the order immediately. This order must be executed at the opening price **only**.

Market On Open This designates your order to be executed as close to the open as possible. It may or may not be the exact opening price, it is only required to be filled as close to the opening price as possible.

Market On Close This qualifier is used frequently with day traders and other short term traders desiring to exit a trade at the close of the market. As with the "market on open" qualifier, the "market on close" qualifier does not guarantee the investor the absolute closing price, but rather a price as near to the closing price as possible. In reality, the investor may receive the actual closing price, but it not guaranteed. The only guarantee is that the order **will be executed**.

SELLING SHORT

There is one other type of order which we have saved for last. This order is termed a "short sale." Selling a stock, or for that matter any other security short, involves borrowing the security from someone else, with the promise of returning that exact security at some later date. In reality, the investor is not really borrowing the security from another person, but rather, from the brokerage firm who in turn borrow's from the customer. Why sell short? Well, short selling has several uses, but its primary use is to allow investors to take a position in the financial markets which will yield financial gain if that particular security should fall in price. For example, assume you had some reason to believe a television, exactly the same as the one your friend just purchased, was going on sale for $100 off next week. You could borrow the television from your friend and sell it immediately at the current price of say $500. Next week when the TV goes on sale, you could buy the TV for $400 and subsequently return the newly purchased TV to your friend. Since you sold the original TV for $500 and purchased the same exact TV a week later for $400, you are able to profit by $100 on the transaction, and have just executed in theory, a short sell.

Now lets relate this scenario to a financial or stock situation. Let's assume IBM is trading at bid 95 and ask 95 1/8. After doing your research, you come to the conclusion that IBM is overpriced and will be subject to a price decline in the near future. You want to profit from this decline so you "sell short."

You instruct your broker to sell short 1000 shares of IBM at the market (current price). Your broker informs you that you have executed your short sell at 95. Now again, what this means is that you have sold to someone in the marketplace, 1000 shares of IBM, shares which you do not own, but rather, have borrowed. Since you have sold the shares, the $95,000 has been deposited in your account, however, this is not really your money because at some time you will have to buy those IBM shares back to return them to the lender.

Over the next 2 or 3 weeks, your analysis proves to be correct, and IBM's price starts to decline. You wait patiently until it reaches the price where you believe it has hit bottom. At this point, the price of IBM is 88 1/2. You call your broker and instruct him/her to **buy the shares "back" to cover the short** (the language used in the industry). Your broker informs you that you have "covered" your IBM short sell at 88 1/2. What has happened from the purchase. The purchase cost you $88,500 (1000 shares at 88 1/2). Conversely, the sell yielded you proceeds of $95,000. Therefore, taking the proceeds from the sale, and subtracting the cost of the purchase, the transaction has produced a net profit for you of $6,500 (Of course this is an approximation because in the real world you would incur other incremental charges such a commissions and possibly dividend charges).

It should also be noted, that not all stocks are available to be sold short. Your broker will be able to inform you as to which stocks may or may not be available for short selling. Also, all short sells must be effected in a "margin" account, and are not usually recommended for the novice or beginning investor.

HOW TO READ THE FINANCIAL NEWSPAPERS

While many do not have access to electronic sources of financial information, most all should have access to printed sources; local papers, *Wall Street Journal* and *Investor Business Daily* just to name a few.

We will begin with the NYSE Composite transactions. (Exhibit 1) It is called "composite" because it includes all transactions on that particular stock including trades that take place on instinet and other off exchange trading venues. At the risk of stating the obvious, the quotations printed in the newspaper are from the **previous day's close** (If you ever come across a newspaper that has the current days closing information, please apprise the author immediately).

52 Week
Hi-Lo

Let's look at the second stock in the table of exhibit 1. That stock is ABM Industries. Starting at the heading of the first column and moving right to left, we first see the 52 week "HI" and "Lo." This means, ABM Ind. stock, during the last year (52 weeks), had a HI of 29 3/16 and a Lo of 15 1/2. Next is the listing (sometimes abbreviated) of the company's name. Following the company's

Symbol

name we see the company's **symbol**. You should notice that our company's symbol is ABM. This is the official symbol of the company and the one to be used when requesting a quote, company information, or when placing a trade. However, it would be advisable to verify the name with the symbol to help prevent any possible confusion or mixup. One last point on symbols: many newspapers, particularly local papers, do not list the official or correct symbol, instead they sometimes "make up" symbols which looks close to the company's name. This practice causes investors and brokers much unnecessary trouble in trying to locate a particular company. These papers may also not list the correct name, but may substitute an abbreviation which they feel is adequate. Obviously, if they print neither the correct name nor the correct symbol, trying to retrieve information on that particular company could prove to be somewhat challenging. The investor should at least be aware of this potential problem when consulting local papers for stock quote information. Of course, some are better than others. Two national daily financial publications, namely the *Wall Street Journal* and *Investors Business Daily*, while they may abbreviate the company's name, will always print the **official and correct symbol**.

Dividend

Continuing across the top heading, we come to the dividend that is payable from the company. The dividend amount stated is the **annual** dividend, and must therefore be divided by 4, (dividends are generally paid quarterly) to arrive at the amount the investor will receive on a quarterly basis. On our stock ABM, the dividend is $.40 cents, therefore, the investor will receive, $.10 cents per share per quarter.

Yield

In the next column, is the percent (%) yield. The dividend yield is very important in the analysis of stocks for several reasons. First and probably most importantly, the higher the yield, on a relative basis, the more likely an investor is to buy and hold that specific security. Also, if the market as a whole begins to decline, the investor holding the higher yielding security will be buffeted somewhat during that decline. Similarly, other investors who might want to also receive this higher yield, - buy the stock - and either prevent the stock from declining as much as others or possibly even raise the stocks price. As you can see, the dividend yield is a very important factor in stock price stability. To calculate the dividend yield, simply divide the annual payable dividend by the current price of the stock. Again, using our example, ABM pays a dividend of $.40 cents, and a current or closing price of 26 13/16.

$$\frac{40}{26 \ 13/16} = .0149 \text{ or } 1.5\%$$

Looking in our yield column, we can confirm that the yield stated is correct.

PE Ratio

Next in our column is the price to earnings ratio or more commonly referred to as the PE ratio. The PE ratio is a very important number for use in financial analysis of stocks. What this figure tells us is the number of times the current price exceeds the companys' earnings in the last 12 months. In other words, if a company earned

$1.00 the past 12 months, and their stock was trading at $10.00, the company would have a PE ratio of 10, meaning their stock price was trading at **10 times** the company's latest 12 month earnings. Let's look at our company ABM and work through some important mathematical calculations.

ABM has a PE ratio of 23 and a closing price of 26 13/16. Well, since we know the PE and we know the price, we can calculate the latest 12 month earnings. We would simply take the closing price of the stock and divide by the PE ratio:

$$\frac{26\ 13/16}{23} = 1.165 \text{ or } 1.17$$

This calculation tells us that ABM Indus. earned $1.17 per share during its latest 12 months. Now lets switch things around. Assume we knew the earning and the closing price, how could we figure the PE ratio? Very easily, by simply taking once again the closing price, and dividing it by the earnings:

$$\frac{26\ 13/16}{1.17} = 22.91 \text{ or } 23$$

Again, comparing with the table, we see that this is in fact correct. Now the question begs itself; why are PE ratios important? Well let's use ABM's PE of 23 for our example. Assume, while researching XYZ industry, we find approximately 20 company's operating therein. One of those companies just happens to be our ABM. Upon further research, we find that most companies in this industry have PE ratios of between 10 and 13. What does this tell us? Well, it tells us that ABM's stock price is about twice that of comparable companies in the same industry. Now the investor must try to ascertain why this is so. Maybe the company has come out with some new product, or new patent which has caused the market to placed a premium on its stock. Those reasons along with many others might explain the PE differential. However, there may not be a quantifiable reason for this high PE. It might be high due to rumor, pending lawsuit, or some other unsubstantiated claim with respect to the company's future. In this event, an investor might assume that company's stock price is over valued, or artificially high and could take market action to attempt to profit from the coming (in the investors mind) stock price decline. Generally speaking, companies in the same industry, with similar products and services, of comparable size and quality, should have similar PE ratios. If not, it is at least an indication that further investigation or analysis is warranted.

Volume

Next in our table is the volume column. The volume is actually the total sales, or volume traded in the stock on that particular day. This figure includes all buys and sell, it is an all-inclusive figure. The number is usually printed in "**100s**". Looking at our company, ABM, what was the total volume traded for ABM on November 6, 1997? The correct answer is 19,900 shares. As you can see from the chart, the stock traded 199 shares, also remembering this figure is in hundreds, we simply multiply 199 x 100, giving us 19,900 shares. One last point on volume: there are some stocks which have small trade volume, this could be the result of several reasons, however, the salient point here is to inform you that the financial newspapers may print the actual number of shares for these firms. When this occurs, the paper will use some symbol to denote "**actual**" shares traded figure is being used.

**Daily
Hi-Lo**

In the next 2 columns, we once again have the Hi and Lo. Notice however, that the Hi and Lo in the fist 2 column were 52 week data. These Hi and Lo figures are just for this particular day. As you can see, the Hi the high price for ABM, for this specific day was 27. Also the Lo price for the same day was 26 1/2. This tells us that during the trading day of November 6, 1997, ABM's stock price fluctuated a maximum of 1/2 point (fifty cents). This information may be helpful for "day traders" attempting to profit from these daily swings. Also, the investor may analyze the daily price variation in order to assist in the process of determining the optimum price at which to place a stop loss or stop limit order.

Closing Price

Next we find the close column. This is simply the closing price of the stock. The last trade of the day. It could have been a purchase at the ask price, a sell at the bid price, or a trade at some price in between the bid and ask, we do not know. The only thing we do know for sure, is that this was the **last** price at which the stock traded for that specific day. For our stock, we see ABM close at 26 13/16.

Net Change

The last column is the "**net change**" figure. This figure simply tells us how much the stock has increased or decreased in price from the **previous days** close. For our stock, we see that ABM's close of 26 13/16 is down 5/16's from its close on Wednesday November 5, 1997.

**Explanatory
Notes**

As you have been perusing the stock tables in exhibit 1, you may have noticed many stocks have denotations (letters or symbols) either to the left of the quote, or embedded within the quote line itself. These represent pieces of information which are important for the investor to know; such as whether the price is a new 52-week high or low, or if a stock split is pending, as well as many others. These denotations are used to convey this type of information to the investor. For general information purposes, the explanatory notes table for the November 6, 1997 issue of the *Wall Street Journal* is shown in exhibit 2. Take time to familiarize yourself with the denotations and their corresponding footnotes. Be aware that these footnotes are specifically for the *Wall Street Journal*. Other financial newspaper will undoubtedly have footnotes, but generally footnotes are **paper specific**.

BONDS

Bond Name

Now let us look at Exhibit 3, where we have our bond quote listing. The first column is the bond name column, it includes 3 crucial pieces of information. The first piece of information is the issuing company's name or symbol. Second, is the "coupon rate" of the bond. And third, is the maturity date of the bond. The natural question at this point: why is so much information presented in the section reserved for the bond name? All of this information, is sometimes needed to locate the specific bond. On many occasions, bonds are issued with the same coupon rates, or the same date of maturity with different coupon rates. Therefore, to ensure the correct bond is quoted or bought or sold, it is critically important to state all three of these bond identifiers to your broker. Once again they are: the name of the issuing company, the coupon rate, and the date of maturity.

Coupon Rate

Date of Maturity

Current Yield

The next column gives us the "**current yield**." Remember from our section on bond yields, the current yield can be (and usually is) different from the coupon rate and the yield to maturity. The current yield figure is just informing the investor as to the rate of return on this bond as calculated from the previous days close only. No capital gain or loss is considered.

Volume Next we find the volume column. This figure is not quoted in "100s" as in the stock tables, it is a true, actual volume. Looking at the first bond listed in the corporate bond section, we see that the total number of bonds traded on this particular issue was 10. That's it. No tricks. Just 10 of these bonds were bought or sold all day.

Close This item is the same as in the stock tables. It simply represents the closing price of the bond.

Net Change This item is very straightforward, it represents the change in price from the previous day's close.

Just as stock table have explanatory notes, the bond tables have them also. You will find them in exhibit 3A. Explanatory notes are generally located near the securities quote tables. I will not take the time to go over everything in this box, but it is worth mentioning that you should be aware of and familiar with this information.

MUTUAL FUNDS

Net Asset Value (NAV) The first column in our mutual fund table, (exhibit 4) is the **Net Asset Value** or otherwise known as "**NAV.**" This represents the closing price of that particular mutual fund.

Net Change Next is net change. This figure represents the increase or decrease in price from the previous days close.

Investment Objectives The next 2 columns encompass the fund's name and its investment objectives. These two categories are linked together because they are intricately intwined. Usually, mutual fund investors will **first** decide the "**type**" of fund (investment objective) in which they wish to invest.

Once the "**type**" of fund has been chosen, the investor decides **which particular fund** is best suited. You will notice many different two letter denotations under the investment objective column, these represent the numerous types of funds available to the investor, and are explained in the footnotes entitled "Mutual Fund Objectives" in exhibit 5.

Percent Return

The next five columns all relate to the percent return, during different time periods, for that particular fund. You might wonder why mutual fund listings have so many different "percent return" time periods. Traditionally mutual funds have marketed themselves to the public by stating a particular "time period" yield. Over time, different mutual funds added additional time periods (usually time periods that reflected their best performance) and before long, there were many different time durations that appeared along with their corresponding yields. As one might expect, through the years some time periods have been discarded and some have become standard. The year-to-date (YTD), along with the 1 year, 3 year, 5 year, and 10 year yields have become the most standard yield reporting time periods.

Maximum Initial Charge

If you move over one column, you'll find the "maximum initial charge." This charge is important because it informs the investor how much of his/her initial investment will be automatically lost to an "entry fee." In years past, most mutual funds charged an entry fee, usually ranging from 2 percent to 7 or 8 percent. However, within the last 5 to 7 years, there has been an explosion of funds available to investors which do not charge any entry fee. These entry fees are called "**loads**," and hence the funds which do not impose these entry fees are similarly called "**no load**" mutual funds. You should recall this from our previous chapter on mutual funds.

However, one final thought on the subject of "loads." Let's assume you are considering a mutual fund which has listed in its return table a one-year return of 8 percent. Also, assume that fund has a initial load charge of 4 percent. The investor in this example would be sacrificing **50 percent** of the first-year return just for the entry fee. There would have to be an awfully compelling reason to persuade the investor to contribute half of the first year return just for the privilege of investing in this particular fund. Maybe its justified, maybe it isn't. That's for the investor to decide.

Expense Ratio The last column is the expense ratio. Mutual funds differ widely in their cost of operating the fund. It is important to choose a fund with a relatively low expense ratio. Who pays the expenses of the fund; that's right–the investor.

Types of Stockbrokerage Firms

Full Service   Full service firms are also referred to as "full commission" firms. They are called such because they provide stock research, analysis, and recommendations to their clients. They typically have research analysts "in-house," which provide research, analysis, and recommendations to their "sales" force (brokers), and the stockbrokers disseminate this information to their clients. Because they provide these "services," they generally charge a substantially higher commission than their "discount broker" counterparts.

Discount Broker   As the term suggest, "discount brokers" commissions or transaction costs are substantially lower than "full service" brokers. In general, the discount brokerage firm does not staff an "in-house" research department, thereby eliminating a large fixed cost and allowing the discount firm to operate more cost efficiently. Having reduced their fixed overhead cost, these firms passed the savings on to the consumer by dramatically reducing their transaction charges. It took the public time to embrace these firms, but as investors became more comfortable with making their own investment decisions, the number and profitability of these firms increased exponentially. The "discount broker" industry was birthed when the U.S. Congress deregulated the the stockbrokerage industry in 1975.

Deep Discount Brokers   From the discount brokerage industry, came the "**deep discount**" industry. These firms found ways to cut their operating cost even further, and passed the saving on to the consumer. They generally provide very few services and have very few branch offices, but for the investor who needs just an order execution, and very little else, they provide a very valuable service.

Exhibit 1

NEW YORK STOCK EXCHANGE COMPOSITE TRANSACTIONS

Quotations as of 5 p.m. Eastern Time
Thursday, November 6, 1997

-A-A-A-

The Dow Jones Averages Hour by Hour

Following are the Dow Jones averages of INDUSTRIAL, TRANSPORTATION and UTILITY stocks with the total sales of each group for the period included in the chart.

DATE	OPEN	10 AM	11 AM	12 NOON	1 PM	2 PM	3 PM	CLOSE	CHG	%	(THEORETICAL)		(ACTUAL)	
											HIGH*	LOW*	HIGH*	LOW*
30 INDUSTRIALS: (divisor: 0.25450704)														
Nov 6	7692.03	7660.89	7666.78	7649.84	7680.29	7689.37	7660.15	7683.24	− 9.33	−.12	7758.43	7597.78	7708.04	7640.36
Nov 5	7488.15	7686.92	7671.45	7698.71	7742.91	7723.51	7747.33	7692.57	+ 3.44	+.04	7791.78	7628.96	7765.75	7664.57
Nov 4	7674.15	7675.13	7632.40	7664.57	7661.13	7638.79	7674.15	7689.13	+14.74	+.19	7757.15	7583.29	7701.65	7622.33
Nov 3	7443.07	7588.69	7575.18	7603.18	7610.79	7607.35	7607.35	7674.39	+232.31	+3.12	7702.39	7500.28	7674.39	7443.07
Oct 31	7384.62	7455.59	7391.49	7407.70	7402.79	7423.38	7444.05	7442.08	+60.41	+.82	7544.24	7329.61	7495.86	7352.69
20 TRANSPORTATION COS.: (divisor: 0.35171330)														
Nov 6	3207.30	3200.05	3197.03	3197.21	3208.58	3214.44	3205.74	3211.60	+ 4.09	+.13	3234.17	3172.31	3218.71	3189.21
Nov 5	3201.26	3190.45	3189.21	3205.56	3219.77	3213.20	3214.09	3207.51	+ 5.68	+.18	3241.63	3172.15	3227.77	3187.61
Nov 4	3200.07	3199.87	3181.84	3187.79	3187.61	3182.10	3192.05	3201.83	− 1.42	−.04	3225.82	3156.87	3203.78	3178.55
Nov 3	3131.46	3170.20	3176.59	3186.90	3192.76	3193.30	3195.96	3203.25	+71.79	+2.29	3209.65	3141.05	3205.03	3131.46
Oct 31	3092.36	3120.97	3103.74	3107.21	3122.04	3138.21		3131.46	+89.81	+1.29	3162.20	3082.94	3144.61	3092.36
15 UTILITIES: (divisor: 2.2811277)														
Nov 6	244.44	242.89	242.75	242.67	242.94	243.19	242.81	242.89	− 1.81	−.74	244.64	241.22	244.44	242.42
Nov 5	244.94	244.29	244.64	245.25	245.57	244.97	245.25	244.76	− 0.27	−.11	246.84	242.73	246.31	244.23
Nov 4	245.22	244.81	243.99	244.23	244.40	244.10	244.56	244.97	− 0.28	−.11	246.15	242.97	245.22	243.85
Nov 3	242.62	244.23	244.92	245.44	245.41	245.00	245.05	245.23	+ 2.66	+1.10	246.64	243.22	245.74	242.62
Oct 31	241.44	242.40	241.93	242.83	242.86	242.59	242.89	242.59	− 1.26	+.52	244.73	240.53	243.77	241.44
65 STOCKS COMPOSITE AVERAGE: (divisor: 1.45046628)														
Nov 6	2511.83	2502.18	2501.57	2499.29	2511.14	2503.30		2508.90	− 3.49	−0.14	2530.36	2481.79	2515.58	2495.58
Nov 5	2510.53	2506.61	2504.16	2513.85	2525.57	2519.63	2524.45	2512.39	+ 1.55	+0.06	2541.43	2489.55	2532.31	2502.95
Nov 4	2508.98	2507.65	2494.48	2501.96	2501.57	2495.84	2505.19	2510.84	+ 1.81	+0.07	2530.44	2478.22	2511.96	2492.57
Nov 3	2446.72	2484.36	2484.64	2492.87	2495.58	2494.46	2497.61	2509.03	+62.33	+2.55	2517.69	2460.21	2509.03	2446.72
Oct 31	2424.61	2447.02	2430.04	2435.13	2438.10	2441.46	2449.18	2446.68	+22.24	+0.92	2475.42	2411.95	2457.92	2421.08

*a-Actual high or low exceeds theoretical value due to computational method. a-Actual. r-Revised.

-B-B-B-

Continued

Taken from *Wall Street Journal*, November, 1997

Exhibit 2

EXPLANATORY NOTES

The following explanations apply to New York and American exchange listed issues and the Nasdaq Stock Market. NYSE and Amex prices are composite quotations that include trades on the Chicago, Pacific, Philadelphia, Boston and Cincinnati exchanges and reported by the National Association of Securities Dealers.

Boldfaced quotations highlight those issues whose price changed by 5% or more if their previous closing price was $2 or higher.

Underlined quotations are those stocks with large changes in volume, per exchange, compared with the issue's average trading volume. The calculation includes common stocks of $5 a share or more with an average volume over 65 trading days of at least 5,000 shares. The underlined quotations are for the 40 largest volume percentage leaders on the NYSE and the Nasdaq National Market. It includes the 20 largest volume percentage gainers on the Amex.

The 52-week high and low columns show the highest and lowest price of the issue during the preceding 52 weeks plus the current week, but not the latest trading day. These ranges are adjusted to reflect stock payouts of 1% or more, and cash dividends or other distributions of 10% or more.

Dividend/Distribution rates, unless noted, are annual disbursements based on the last monthly, quarterly, semiannual, or annual declaration. Special or extra dividends or distributions, including return of capital, special situations or payments not designated as regular are identified by footnotes.

Yield is defined as the dividends or other distributions paid by a company on its securities, expressed as a percentage of price.

The P/E ratio is determined by dividing the closing market price by the company's primary per-share earnings for the most recent four quarters. Charges and other adjustments usually are excluded when they qualify as extraordinary items under generally accepted accounting rules.

Sales figures are the unofficial daily total of shares traded, quoted in hundreds (two zeros omitted; f-four zeros omitted.)

Exchange ticker symbols are shown for all New York and American exchange common stocks, and Dow Jones News/Retrieval symbols are listed for Class A and Class B shares listed on both markets. Nasdaq symbols are listed for all Nasdaq NMS issues. A more detailed explanation of Nasdaq ticker symbols appears with the NMS listings.

FOOTNOTES: ⬆-New 52-week high. ▼-New 52-week low. a-Extra dividend or extras in addition to the regular dividend. b-Indicates annual rate of the cash dividend and that a stock dividend was paid. c-Liquidating dividend. cc-P/E ratio is 100 or more. dd-Loss in the most recent four quarters. e-Indicates a dividend was declared in the preceding 12 months, but that there isn't a regular dividend rate. Amount shown may have been adjusted to reflect stock split, spinoff or other distribution. ec-Emerging Company Marketplace issue. FD-First day of trading. f-Annual rate, increased on latest declaration. g-Indicates the dividend and earnings are expressed in Canadian money. The stock trades in U.S. dollars. No yield or P/E ratio is shown. gg-Special sales condition; no regular way trading. h-Temporary exemption from Nasdaq requirements. i-Indicates amount declared or paid after a stock dividend or split. j-Indicates dividend was paid this year, and that at the last dividend meeting a dividend was omitted or deferred. k-Indicates dividend declared this year on cumulative issues with dividends in arrears. m-Annual rate, reduced on latest declaration. n-Newly issued in the past 52 weeks. The high-low range begins with the start of trading and doesn't cover the entire period. p-Initial dividend; no yield calculated. pf-Preferred. pp-Holder owes installment(s) of purchase price. pr-Preference. r-Indicates a cash dividend declared in the preceding 12 months, plus a stock dividend. rt-Rights. s-Stock split or stock dividend, or cash or cash equivalent distribution, amounting to 10% or more in the past 52 weeks. The high-low price is adjusted from the old stock. Dividend calculations begin with the date the split was paid or the stock dividend occurred. stk-Paid in stock in the last 12 months. Company doesn't pay cash dividend. un-Units. v-Trading halted on primary market. vi-In bankruptcy or receivership or being reorganized under the Bankruptcy Code, or securities assumed by such companies. wd-When distributed. wi-When issued. wt-Warrants. ww-With warrants. x-Ex-dividend, ex-distribution, ex-rights or without warrants. z-Sales in full, not in 100s.

Exhibit 3

C20 THE WALL STREET JOURNAL FRIDAY, NOVEMBER 7, 1997

NEW YORK EXCHANGE BONDS

Quotations as of 4 p.m. Eastern Time
Thursday, November 6, 1997

Volume $18,355,000

	Domestic		All Issues	
	Thu.	Wed.	Thu.	Wed.
Issues traded	249	262	255	269
Advances	115	128	118	133
Declines	88	88	91	89
Unchanged	46	46	46	47
New highs	13	13	13	13
New lows	3	4	3	5

SALES SINCE JANUARY 1
(000 omitted)

1997	1996	1995
$4,455,404	$4,831,556	$6,226,151

Dow Jones Bond Averages

	1996		1997			1997		1996	
	High	Low	High	Low		Close	Chg. %Yld	Close	Chg.
106.09	100.99	104.70	101.09	20 Bonds	104.33	+0.07	6.98	103.43	+0.05
102.43	97.46	102.38	97.64	10 Utilities	102.01	−0.06	6.99	100.56	+0.02
109.94	104.06	107.23	104.54	10 Industrials	106.66	+0.22	6.97	106.30	+0.08

CORPORATION BONDS
Volume, $17,888,000

Exhibit 3A

EXPLANATORY NOTES
(For New York and American Bonds)
Yield is Current yield.
cv-Convertible bond. cf-Certificates.
cld-Called. dc-Deep discount. ec-European currency units. f-Dealt in flat.
li-Italian lire. kd-Danish kroner. m-Matured bonds, negotiability impaired by maturity. na-No accrual. r-Registered.
rp-Reduced principal. st, sd-Stamped.
t-Floating rate. wd-When distributed.
ww-With warrants. x-Ex interest.
xw-Without warrants. zr-Zero coupon.
vj-In bankruptcy or receivership or being reorganized under the Bankruptcy Act, or securities assumed by such companies.

Taken from *Wall Street Journal*, November, 1997

Exhibit 4

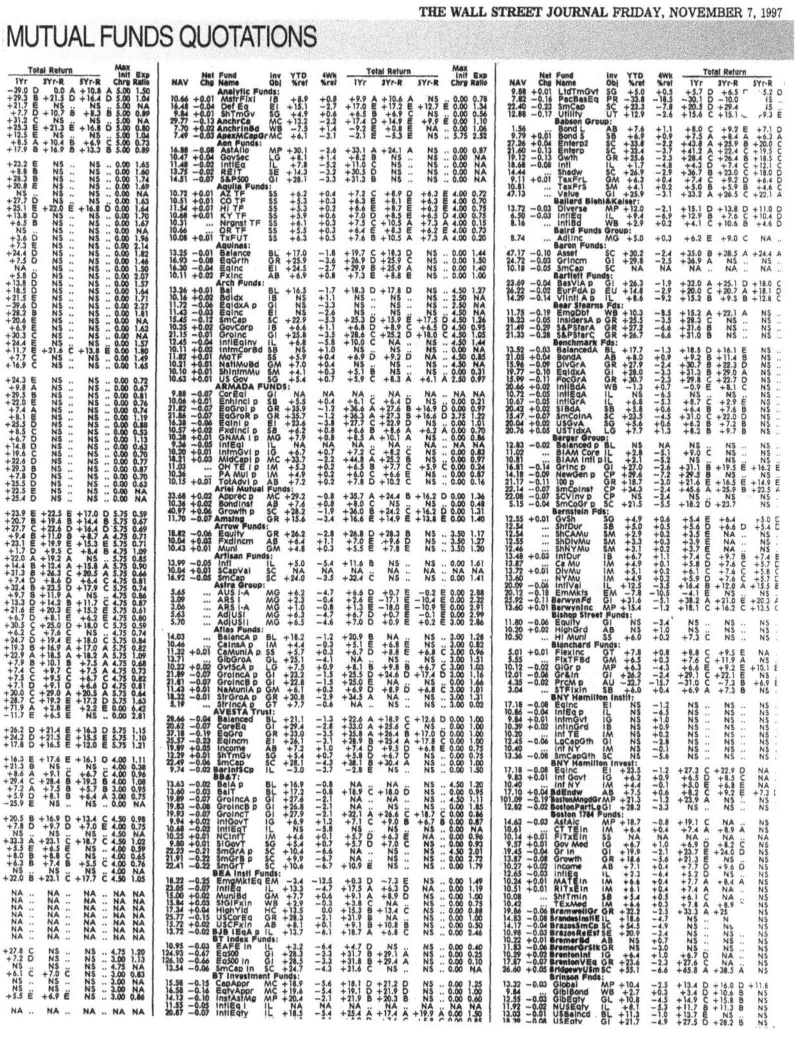

THE WALL STREET JOURNAL FRIDAY, NOVEMBER 7, 1997

MUTUAL FUNDS QUOTATIONS

Taken from *Wall Street Journal*, November, 1997

Exhibit 5

MUTUAL FUND OBJECTIVES

Categories compiled by The Wall Street Journal, based on classifications by Lipper Analytical Services Inc.

STOCK FUNDS

Capital Appreciation (CP): Seeks rapid capital growth, often through high portfolio turnover.

Growth (GR): Invests in companies expecting higher than average revenue and earnings growth.

Growth & Income (GI): Pursues both price and dividend growth. Category includes S&P 500 index funds.

Equity Income (EI): Tends to favor stock with the highest dividends.

Small Cap (SC): Stocks of lesser-known, small companies.

MidCap (MC): Shares of middle-sized companies.

Sector (SE): Environmental; Financial Services; Real Estate; Specialty & Miscellaneous.

Global Stock (GL): Includes small cap global. Can invest in U.S.

International Stock (IL) (non-U.S.): Canadian; International; International Small Cap.

European Region (EU): European markets or operations concentrated in Europe.

Latin America (LT): Markets or operations concentrated in Latin America.

Pacific Region (PR): Japanese; Pacific Ex-Japan; Pacific Region; China Region.

Emerging Markets (EM): Emerging market equity securities (based on economic measures such as a country's GNP per capita).

Science & Technology (TK): Science, technology and telecommunications stocks.

Health & Biotechnology (HB): Health care, medicine and biotechnology.

Natural Resources (NR): Natural resources stocks.

Gold (AU): Gold mines, gold-oriented mining finance houses, gold coins or bullion.

Utility (UT): Utility stocks.

TAXABLE BOND FUNDS

Short-Term (SB): Ultrashort obligation and short, short-intermediate investment grade corporate debt.

Short-Term U.S. (SG): Short-term U.S. Treasury; Short, short-intermediate U.S. government funds.

Intermediate (IB): Investment grade corporate debt of up to 10-year maturity.

Intermediate U.S. (IG): U.S. Treasury and government agency debt.

Long-Term (AB): Corporate A-rated; Corporate BBB-rated.

Long-Term U.S. (LG): U.S. Treasury; U.S. government; zero coupon.

General U.S. Taxable (GT): Can invest in different types of bonds.

High Yield Taxable (HC): High yield high-risk bonds.

Mortgage (MG): Ginnie Mae and general mortgage; Adjustable-Rate Mortgage.

World (WB): Short world multi-market; short world single-market; global income; international income; Emerging-Markets debt.

MUNICIPAL BOND FUNDS

Short-Term Muni (SM): Short, short-intermediate municipal debt; Short-Intermediate term California; Single states short-intermediate municipal debt.

Intermediate Muni (IM): Intermediate-term municipal debt including single-state funds.

General Muni (GM): A variety of municipal debt.

Single-State Municipal (SS): Funds that invest in debt of individual states.

High Yield Municipal (HM): High yield low credit quality.

Insured (NM): California insured, New York insured, Florida insured, all other insured.

STOCK & BOND FUNDS

Balanced (BL): A balanced portfolio of both stocks and bonds with the primary objective of conserving principal.

Stock/Bond Blend (MP): Multi-purpose funds such as balanced target; convertible; flexible income; flexible portfolio; global flexible and income funds that invest in both stocks and bonds.

Taken from *Wall Street Journal*, November, 1997

6

Margin

"...Shallow men believe in luck,... strong believe in cause and effect..."

Ralph Waldo Emerson
(1808-1882)
American essayist and poet

MARGIN

In our previous discussion of securities markets, we learned how and where securities are bought and sold as well as the many different types of orders available to help the investor meet their specific needs. In most of our discussion, we assumed that the investor was purchasing stock, and paying for the purchase in full. Well, this is not always the case. In our societal age of borrowing money, there is, as you might expect, an avenue available for the investor to borrow money from the brokerage firm to buy various securities. In our discussion of margin, we will concentrate on the use of margin (or borrowing) in purchasing stocks. While the subject can be very complex, we will focus only on the basics for a general understanding.

Regulation T   The use of credit for purchasing securities is governed by "**Regulation T**" of the Securities Exchange Act of 1934. Reg T, empowers the Federal Reserve Board to set standards governing margin transactions. One such standard set by the Federal Reserve Board, is the percentage of down payment the investor must make when initiating a margin transaction. This "down payment" percentage is commonly known and referred to as "**Reg T.**" Reg T is currently 50%, and has been since January 1974. However, it is important to realize that Reg T can be raised or lowered by the Federal Reserve Board whenever deemed appropriate.

Margin
Account   A margin account is an account opened by the customer for the expressed purpose of buying securities with borrowed money from the brokerage firm. You should also know that having a margin account does not mandate the use of its borrowing capabilities. If you purchase stock on margin, you can always pay for your transaction in full by the settlement date and no interest will be charged. With the account, however, the investor has the

choice of paying anywhere between the minimum of 50% to the maximum of 100% of the transactions.

Margin Agreement

Before a brokerage firm can lend money to any investor, the law requires the loan to be secured or collateralized. In order to satisfy this legal requirement, the customer must sign a legal document which, in effect, states that the customer agrees to pledge any securities purchased as collateral for the brokerage firm's loan. This legal document is known as a "**margin agreement**."

Hypothecation

Under this agreement, the customer formally and legally pledges the purchased securities as collateral for the loan. The act of pledging securities for a brokerage firm loan is called "**hypothecation**". The customer has "hypothecated" (pledged) his/her securities purchased as collateral for the loan.

Rehypothecation

Rehypothecation, is the act of the brokerage firm pledging customers securities as collateral to secure loans from banks. The loans the brokerage firm receives from the banks are used to finance the margin loan request from the firms customers. The customer gives the brokerage firm the authority to re-pledge or rehypothecate customer securities to banks through the signing of the margin account agreement.

Street Name

If a customer wishes to invest on margin, the securities must be held in the brokerage firm's name. Shares held by the brokerage firm in their name are referred to as being held in "**street name**." It is important, for the brokerage firm, that the shares be held in street name because should a problem arise with respect to payment from the customer, it facilitates the brokerage firms ability to liquidate the securities.

Beneficial Owner   The beneficial owner is the actual customer who purchased the securities. Although the securities are registered in the brokerage firm's name (street name) the beneficial owner is the brokerage firm's customer. This means that **all benefits** of ownership, such as dividends or interest, capital appreciation, voting rights, pre-emptive rights, and the right to sell the total position, reside and remain with the actual customer.

Debit Balance   The debit balance is the amount of the loan which the customer has received from the brokerage firm. If the investor purchased $10,000 in stock, and deposited $6,000 in cash, the brokerage firm would lend the remaining $4,000.00 to the investor. This $4,000 is termed the **debit balance**. If the investor deposited another $2,000 two weeks later, it would automatically be applied to the current debit balance resulting in a new debit balance of $2,000.

Current Market Value   The current market value is exactly what is states. It is the market value of the securities in the account usually calculated from the previous days closing prices. The current market value (CMV) is used extensively in calculating most margin applications.

Equity   The equity calculation in securities, is the same as in your home. The value of your home less your mortgage, gives you your equity. Similarly, the value of your securities (CMV) less your borrowed money (debit balance) gives you your equity.

Before we go any further, this seems like a good place to work through a few examples on margin basics.

INITIAL MARGIN CALL AND EQUITY

In our examples, Reg T is 50%.   Assume the following:

> A customer purchases 100 shares of IBM at $100 per share in a margin account. What is the required initial margin deposit (also referred to as a "Fed Call" or "initial call").

We find the initial margin call by multiplying the total amount of the purchase by Reg T. Hence,

> 100 shares x $100 per share = $10,000.00 Total Pur.

> $10,000.00 x .50 (Reg T) = $5,000.00 Initial Margin
>   Requirement

> What is the customers equity? We always find the customers equity by using the following formula:

> | | |
> |---|---|
> | CMV (current market value) | $10,000 |
> | - DR   (Debit Balance) | $5,000 |
> | Equity | $5,000 |

> What would the equity be if IBM increased to 110 per share?

> | | |
> |---|---|
> | CMV | 11,000 |
> | - DR | - 5,000 |
> | Equity | 6,000 |

What would be the equity if IBM decreased to 83 per share?

CMV	8,300
- DR	- 5,000
Equity	3,300

Maintenance Call

Naturally, since your securities are pledged collateral for your brokerage loan, the firm will not allow your securities to decline substantially in value without requesting that you deposit additional money. This request is termed a "**maintenance call**." Every brokerage firm has a "set" percentage of equity which the customer must maintain. Because this percentage can differ from firm to firm, this percentage is called the "house" maintenance. Usually, this house maintenance is set at 35%, but as stated earlier, it can differ from firm to firm. When the value of margined securities declines, so does the investors equity. When this equity declines below a certain "set" percentage, the firm issues the account a statement demanding additional funds be deposited. Again, this demand for additional funds is a "maintenance call." It is important to distinguish between and understand the two types of of "money calls" an investor could receive when utilizing a margin account. The first, is the initial deposit after the purchase. This is called a "**Fed Call**," after the initial deposit, any subsequent requests for money are "**maintenance calls**."

BUYING POWER AND FREE CASH

Buying power and free cash are two subjects which one could complicate ad infinitum. For our discussion, we will simply attempt to give the reader a basic understanding of how these two items are used and how they are derived. With that as our premise, let us proceed.

Excess Equity Buying Power and free cash are functions of "**excess equity**." Excess equity is defined as the amount of equity in the account over and above the required house equity level. If you recall from our discussion on maintenance, the brokerage firm will demand that the investor deposit more money if the value of the securities drops below a specified point. What happens if the value of the securities rises? The amount that the investor has borrowed from the firm, (the debit balance) **always** remains the same (barring of course the additional deposit of money). Therefore, the account value (equity) will decrease if the value of the securities are decreasing, and increase if the value of the securities are increasing. When the value is increasing, the investor will realize what is called "**excess equity**." What can the investor do with excess equity? Several things. First, the investor could opt to do nothing. Secondly, the investor could decide to withdraw any portion or all of the "**Free Cash**" created by the excess equity. Thirdly, the investor could decide to purchase additional securities with the "**Buying Power**" created by the excess equity.

Let's look at a mathematical example to help clarify these topics.

Always remember this formula:

Actual Equity - Required Equity = Excess Equity

(If this formula produces a negative number, a maintenance call for that amount would be generated)

Also, let's continue to use our previous example of an investor purchasing 100 shares of IBM at $100 on margin.

Purchase cost   = $10,000
Fed Call (Reg T) = $ 5,000

Equity $ 5,000

Also assume that the Reg T requirement is 50% and the house or maintenance requirement is 35%.

Required Reg T equity is 50% or 5,000. If the securities should increase in value to $110 per share the account valued as:

CMV	$11,000	100 shares x 110 per share
Debit	$ 5,000	initial loan from brokerage firm
Actual Equity	$6,000	
- Required Equity	$5,000	(Reg T)
Excess Equity	$1,000	

This $1,000 of excess equity will create $1,000 of **"Buying Power."** This means, the investor could now decide to purchase additional securities worth $1,000 dollars without depositing any additional money. The rise in account value has created excess equity, which in turn, has created buying power. When an account value increases above the Reg T requirement, excess equity and buying power are created. Conversely, when an account value decreases below the house maintenance requirement, a maintenance call is created.

Free Cash

To explain free cash, we must return to our Reg T percentage of 50%. Again, this means that the brokerage firm is allowed to lend the investor a maximum of 50% of the value of securities held in the account. In the above example, we have $1,000 of excess equity; or another way to say the same thing is that we have $1000 dollars worth of securities which have no loan attached to them as yet. Since these securities are worth $1,000, and Reg T allows the firm to lend up to 50% of the value of securities (for initial purchases), the firm could legally lend the investor $500 on the $1000 of excess equity now present in the account. This $500 figure is aptly termed "**Free Cash**." However, it is not free. Should the investor decide to withdraw this money, or utilize the free cash by purchasing additional securities with buying power, the brokerage firm will immediately begin charging the investor interest. The investor should also be aware that **interest income** is a huge profit center for larger brokerage firms. In conclusion, let me reiterate that although this is a very brief and simplistic analysis of buying power and free cash, it does provide the investor a basic understanding of how they work, particularly, in relation to accounts.

NYSE/NASD Minimum Credit Requirement

This rule states that no brokerage firm can lend any money to any investor whose margin account does not have, at a minimum, $2,000 of equity. Also, the investor cannot buy on margin unless the purchase is more than $2,000. Again let's look at few examples to further clarify these rules.

Example 1) A customer buy 100 shares of a $15 stock in a margin account. What amount must the investor deposit?

Answer: $1500. The total purchase is below the minimum $2,000 level, therefore the full purchase price must be paid.

Example 2) A customer buy 300 shares at $20 per share. How much must the customer deposit.

Answer: $3,000. The total purchase amount of $6,000 is

above the $2,000 minimum, therefore, the customer is required to deposit $2,000 or 50% of the purchase, whichever is greater.

Example 3) A customer buy 200 shares at $18 per share. What is the customers initial Fed Call?

Answer: $2000. The total purchase price is $3,600. 50% would be $1800 which is below our $2,000 minimum equity requirement. Therefore the customer would be required to deposit $2,000.

Important Points To Remember

1) A customer is never called upon to pay more than the purchase price.

2) A customer cannot be granted any loans until his/her account equity has a minimum of $2,000.

3) If a decline in market value brings the equity below $2,000, no additional funds are required to reestablish the account at minimum equity levels, as long as the account remains above the "House" maintenance level.

7

Securities Analysis

"...Nothing in this world can take the place
of persistence. Talent will not; nothing
is more common than unsuccessful men
of talent. Genius will not... the world is full of
educated derelicts. The slogan "Press on" has
solved and always will solve the problems of
the human race..."

Calvin Coolidge
(1872-1933)
30th president of the United States

SECURITIES ANALYSIS

Securities analysis concerns itself with the evaluation of securities. There are various types of evaluations, and also various types of risks associated with securities investments. In this section we will attempt to identify, define, and explain these varying types of risks, and the methods of evaluations used to try and control these risks.

RISK

Risk

Risk is many things to many people. Not only people, but corporations have to plan for the inevitable and inescapable phenomenon we call Risk. What is risk? *Webster's* defines risk as, "the possibility of loss or injury", "a dangerous element or factor", and "to expose to hazard or danger". From these definitions it is very obvious that risk is **not a good thing**. Because of the inherent "badness" of risk, human beings, corporations, and other institutions have been trying to find ways to accurately measure risk in the hope of ultimately being able to control the exposure to risk, thereby alleviating if not eliminating the perils of risk. For our purposes, we will combine parts of *Webster's* definition to arrive at the following:

Risk– a dangerous element or hazard causing the possibility of loss or injury.

In any analysis of securities, the investor needs to be aware of the various types of risks. By obtaining this understanding, he or she will be much more able to evaluate and control risk exposure.

Any investment is made with the expectation of a return. When an investor makes an investment, he or she assesses the risk then assigns a required "fee." This fee is the "return on investment." Subsequently, risk and return have developed a direct and proportional relationship. The greater the perceived risk, the greater the required return. The lower the perceived risk, the lower the required return. This is the fundamental relationship between risk and return. Now let us take a look at the various types of risk present in the financial marketplace.

Systematic Risk

Systematic risk is the risk of something happening that will adversely effect all securities in a particular class in the same manner. For example, the possibility that the federal government will raise taxes on cigarettes, is a systematic risk. This would undoubtedly have an adverse effect on all cigarette manufacturers. About all you can do to temper systematic risk is try to assess which securities will be most or least affected and allocate your resources accordingly.

Market Risk

Systematic risk is also referred to as "**market risk**." Market risk has to do with, as the name suggest, risk associated with the market in general. For example, if you purchased a stock a week before the stock market crash of 1987, you would have–most likely–lost money even though your particular stock might have had good news that day and might have been defensive in nature. Your loss would have been due, not to your particular stock, but rather to the market itself. This is the essence of market risk, the risk that something will adversely effect the entire market.

Unsystematic Risk

Unsystematic risk relates to those risks which are specific to a particular issuer or company rather than to the market as a whole. This type of risk is also referred to as "**business risk**". Business risk is defined as the uncertainty that the specific issuer whose securities you have purchased will not perform according to expectations.

Credit Risk   Just as with business risk, credit risk is specific to the particular issuer. Credit risk is primarily concerned with the issuers ability to repay interest and principal in a timely manner. Several companies exist today to assist the investing public as to the credit worthiness of individual companies, two of the most well known are "Standard & Poors", and "Moody's."

Inflation Risk   Inflation risk is the risk that our "dollar" may not be able purchase, in the future, the same amount of goods and services it purchases today. As prices rise, we are able to buy less and less with the same amount of money. This increase in prices is called "inflation". Inflation risk is also sometimes referred to as **"purchasing power risk."**

Interest Rate Risk   This type of risk is based on the possibility that interest rates will rise and subsequently cause a reduction in the value of our securities portfolio. Debt securities have the greatest exposure to interest rate risk. As mentioned previously, debt securities prices tend to rise when interest rates fall, and fall when interest rates rise. Debt securities and interest rates have an **"inverse"** relationship. Interest rate risk is also known as **"money rate risk."**

Liquidity Risk   Liquidity risk is the risk that there may not be a viable market in which to buy or sell securities. In some securities, trading is of a particularly low volume. Because of this low volume, the bid ask spread would be wider than on other higher volume securities. This causes the average investor, to buy at higher prices and sell at lower prices than would otherwise be necessary. If an investor is considering purchasing a security with a low trading volume, performing a liquidity risk analysis is crucial.

Legislative Risk   This is the risk that legislative changes, or **changes in the law**, will have a detrimental effect on your portfolio.

The changes could be tax law changes, antitrust action, or even the outright banning of a particular product. Because of the various risk encompassed in legislative risk, it can be said to be **both systematic and unsystematic**.

Call Risk   This risk is associated with primarily debt securities and debt similar securities such as preferred stocks. This is the risk that your security could be "**called**" at a pre-specified price. A security can only be called, after the pre-set date and at or above the pre-specified price. The corporation will call a security only if there is a legal right and an economic benefit in doing so.

Timing Risk   This type of risk could be described as just "bad luck" risk. If your purchased securities a few days before the 1987 stock market crash, your timing was - needless to say–not the best, and it is safe to say you were a victim of "**timing risk**." Timing risk is a form of systematic and market risk.

Now that we have an understanding of the perils that await us in the investing marketplace, let's examine the two primary theories of security analysis. They are:

1) Fundamental Analysis
2) Technical Analysis

It is often suggested that fundamental analysis concerns itself with "**which**" company to invest in, while technical analysis is about "**when**" to invest. While I do agree with the premise of this statement, its scope is much too simplistic because from time to time, these two do tend to overlap and even supplant one another. Determining which one is better, is the subject of much debate. After this section you, too, will undoubtedly join the discussion and debate.

FUNDAMENTAL ANALYSIS

During our discussion of fundamental analysis, we will concentrate on the goals of fundamental analysis and the tools used to reach those goals. We will try, as much as possible, to eliminate most of the mathematical computations. However, it will be necessary to illustrate a few for clarification purposes.

Fundamental Factors
Fundamental analysis deals with the "fundamental" factors of the company. A few primary factors are listed below. However, this list is not exhaustive.

- The outlook for the industry
- The management of the company
- The product lines of the company
- Anticipated future product lines
- Market share of the company

While the above listed factors are mostly "qualitative" in scope, the fundamental analyst uses "quantitative" measurements to evaluate and hopefully answer qualitative questions. For the remainder of our discussion on fundamental analysis, we will review these quantitative analysis tools.

Financial Statements
The primary resource tools of financial analysts are the financial statements. The two primary statements are:

- The Balance Sheet
- The Income Statement

Balance Sheet
If you have ever applied for a loan, you undoubtedly recall the financial institution requiring you to list all of your debt obligations (bills), along with the property you owned (i.e. cars, boats, homes, etc.). Once you completed this task, (and for most of us it is a task) you had

essentially prepared the equivalent of your own personal balance sheet. A balance sheet, therefore, is simply a statement of a corporation's assets and liabilities at a specific point in time.

Income Statement

Every time we prepare our 1040 tax returns we are, in effect, preparing and submitting to the IRS an income statement. A corporate income statement is essentially the same. It will list all income the corporation has realized for that specific reporting period, along with certain other cost or expenses, to derive what is ultimately the net income of the corporations.

From this point forward, we will review the various methods used by financial analysts to evaluate the **relative** strength or weakness of a particular company.

Balance Sheet Formula

The formula for the balance sheet is:

Assets - Liabilities = Net Worth

By rearranging the items, the formula becomes:

Assets = Liabilities + Net Worth

The asset side of the balance sheet is arranged in order of "liquidity." Those assets that are quickly convertible into cash are listed first. Going down the sheet, the assets become less and less liquid. Similarly, the liabilities side of the balance sheet is also arranged in order of liquidity–those liabilities which must be paid promptly, are listed first. Longer term liabilities are listed next, and finally, after all liabilities, the stockholders equity section is listed, sometimes under the term "net worth."

ABC CORPORATION
BALANCE SHEET   EXHIBIT 1

Current Assets:

Cash	$25,000
Accounts Receivable	18,000
Inventory	35,000
Securities	17,000
Total Current Assets	$95,000

Current Liabilities:

Accounts Payable	$15,000
Bank Loan	12,000
Accrued Expense	3,000
Total Current Liabilities	$30,000
Mortgage Bond	110,000
Total Liabilities	$140,000

Fixed Assets:

Plant & Equip.	$300,000	
Less: Depreciation	85,000	
Net Property		215,000
Land		65,000
Goodwill		20,000
Total Assets		$395,000

Capital and Surplus:

Capital Stock	
Preferred Stock, 5% ($25 Par)	
1,000 shares outstanding	$25,000
Common Stock, ($20 Par)	
6,000 shares outstanding	$120,000
Surplus:	
Capital	$30,000
Earned	$80,000

Market Price: $40.00 per share

Total Stockholders Equity $255,000

INCOME STATEMENT   EXHIBIT 2

Net Sales:		$150,000
Cost and Expenses		
Cost of Good Sold	$70,000	
Selling Expense	$15,000	
Depreciation	$10,000	
Maintenance	$20,000	
Property Taxes	$ 5,000	$120,000
Operating Profit:		30,000
Interest:		8,000
Income Before Federal Income Tax		$ 22,000
Federal Income Tax		4,000
Net Income		$ 18,000

Statement of Changes to Retained Earnings

Earned Surplus, Dec. 31 (previous year)	$73,000	
Preferred Dividend: $2.00 per share	$ 2,000	
Common Dividend: $1.50 per share	$ 9,000	$ 11,000
Balance Carried To Earned Surplus		7,000
Previous Surplus, Dec. 31 (previous year)		$ 73,000
Earned Surplus, December 31 (current year)		$ 80,000

In order to give you a working knowledge of the primary fundamental analysis tools, it is necessary to review and become familiar with a sample balance sheet and income statement. Because it is not my intent to make you a financial analyst, but rather to educate and familiarize you with the basic fundamental procedures of analyses, I will utilize somewhat rudimentary financial statements. While this should make our analyses somewhat easier to work through and understand, it does not diminish the lessons which should be learned from the mathematical exercises.

For the duration of our discussion on balance sheets and income statements and the math applications which follow, we will utilize the financial information contained in exhibits 1and 2 for ABC Co.

CURRENT ASSETS AND LIABILITIES

Current Assets The "current" section of the balance sheet is used to evaluate the "liquidity" of the corporation. An item is considered "current" if it comes due within one year.

Current assets includes the following:
1) Cash and Marketable Securities
2) Accounts receivables
3) Inventory

Current Liabilities Current liabilities include the following:
1) Accounts payable
2) Wages payable
3) Taxes payable
4) Interest payable

The above listed accounts included in current assets and liabilities are not exhaustive but are typical. The salient point to derive from this review of current accounts, is

ABC CORPORATION
BALANCE SHEET   EXHIBIT 1

Current Assets:			Current Liabilities:	
Cash	$25,000		Accounts Payable	$15,000
Accounts Receivable	18,000		Bank Loan	12,000
Inventory	35,000		Accrued Expense	3,000
Securities	17,000		**Total Current Liabilities**	$30,000
Total Current Assets	$95,000			
			Mortgage Bond	110,000
			Total Liabilities	$140,000

Fixed Assets:			Capital and Surplus:	
Plant & Equip.	$300,000		Capital Stock	
Less: Depreciation	85,000		Preferred Stock, 5% ($25 Par)	
Net Property	215,000		1,000 shares outstanding	$25,000
Land	65,000		Common Stock, ($20 Par)	
Goodwill	20,000		6,000 shares outstanding	$120,000
Total Assets	$395,000		Surplus:	
			Capital	$30,000
			Earned	$80,000
Market Price: $40.00 per share			**Total Stockholders Equity**	$255,000

INCOME STATEMENT   EXHIBIT 2

Net Sales:		$150,000
Cost and Expenses		
Cost of Good Sold	$70,000	
Selling Expense	$15,000	
Depreciation	$10,000	
Maintenance	$20,000	
Property Taxes	$ 5,000	$120,000
Operating Profit:		30,000
Interest:		8,000
Income Before Federal Income Tax		$ 22,000
Federal Income Tax		4,000
Net Income		$ 18,000

Statement of Changes to Retained Earnings

Earned Surplus, Dec. 31 (previous year)	$73,000	
Preferred Dividend: $2.00 per share	$ 2,000	
Common Dividend: $1.50 per share	$ 9,000	$ 11,000
Balance Carried To Earned Surplus		7,000
Previous Surplus, Dec. 31 (previous year)		$ 73,000
Earned Surplus, December 31 (current year)		$ 80,000

that they include all obligations or assets **which become due or can be liquidated within one year**.

Now let us review some "current account" math applications.

ABC CORPORATION
BALANCE SHEET   EXHIBIT 1

Current Assets:			Current Liabilities:	
Cash	$25,000		Accounts Payable	$15,000
Accounts Receivable	18,000		Bank Loan	12,000
Inventory	35,000		Accrued Expense	3,000
Securities	17,000		**Total Current Liabilities**	$30,000
Total Current Assets	$95,000			
			Mortgage Bond	110,000
			Total Liabilities	$140,000

Fixed Assets:			Capital and Surplus:	
Plant & Equip.	$300,000		Capital Stock	
Less: Depreciation	85,000		Preferred Stock, 5% ($25 Par)	
Net Property	215,000		1,000 shares outstanding	$25,000
Land	65,000		Common Stock, ($20 Par)	
Goodwill	20,000		6,000 shares outstanding	$120,000
Total Assets	$395,000		Surplus:	
			Capital	$30,000
			Earned	$80,000
Market Price: $40.00 per share			**Total Stockholders Equity**	$255,000

INCOME STATEMENT   EXHIBIT 2

Net Sales:		$150,000
Cost and Expenses		
Cost of Good Sold	$70,000	
Selling Expense	$15,000	
Depreciation	$10,000	
Maintenance	$20,000	
Property Taxes	$ 5,000	$120,000
Operating Profit:		30,000
Interest:		8,000
Income Before Federal Income Tax		$ 22,000
Federal Income Tax		4,000
Net Income		$ 18,000

Statement of Changes to Retained Earnings

Earned Surplus, Dec. 31 (previous year)	$73,000	
Preferred Dividend: $2.00 per share	$ 2,000	
Common Dividend: $1.50 per share	$ 9,000	$ 11,000
Balance Carried To Earned Surplus		7,000
Previous Surplus, Dec. 31 (previous year)		$ 73,000
Earned Surplus, December 31 (current year)		$ 80,000

The following ratios are used to measure liquidity.

Working Capital

Working Capital is computed by taking the current assets and subtracting out current liabilities.

Current Assets - Current Liabilities = Working Capital

Referring act to ABC Co.(exhibit 1), the working capital would be 65,000. (95,000 - 30,000)

Working capital is the amount of short-term money available to the corporation for continuing operations. Assume company A has 50 million in working capital and company B has 5 million in working capital. Which company is in better financial shape. If you answered company A, that would be incorrect. We must analyze further in order to accurately answer this question. Upon further analysis, we discover the following:

	Company A	Company B
Current Assets	$900,000,000	$7,500,000
Current Liabilities	$850,000,000	$2,500,000
Working Capital	$ 50,000,000	$5,000,000

With this additional information, we can now answer the question. The answer is obviously Company B. Proper analysis of liquidity requires that we compute the "relationship" between current assets and current liabilities. This **relationship** is called the "**Current Ratio**."

Current Ratio

Again, the ratio measures the relationship between current assets and current liabilities. The formula is:

$$\frac{\text{Current Assets}}{\text{Current Liabilities}} = \text{Current Ratio}$$

ABC CORPORATION
BALANCE SHEET   EXHIBIT 1

Current Assets:			Current Liabilities:	
Cash	$25,000		Accounts Payable	$15,000
Accounts Receivable	18,000		Bank Loan	12,000
Inventory	35,000		Accrued Expense	3,000
Securities	17,000		**Total Current Liabilities**	$30,000
Total Current Assets	$95,000			
			Mortgage Bond	110,000
			Total Liabilities	$140,000

Fixed Assets:			Capital and Surplus:	
Plant & Equip.	$300,000		Capital Stock	
Less: Depreciation	85,000		Preferred Stock, 5% ($25 Par)	
Net Property	215,000		1,000 shares outstanding	$25,000
Land	65,000		Common Stock, ($20 Par)	
Goodwill	20,000		6,000 shares outstanding	$120,000
Total Assets	$395,000		Surplus:	
			Capital	$30,000
			Earned	$80,000
Market Price: $40.00 per share			**Total Stockholders Equity**	$255,000

INCOME STATEMENT   EXHIBIT 2

Net Sales:		$150,000
Cost and Expenses		
Cost of Good Sold	$70,000	
Selling Expense	$15,000	
Depreciation	$10,000	
Maintenance	$20,000	
Property Taxes	$ 5,000	$120,000
Operating Profit:		30,000
Interest:		8,000
Income Before Federal Income Tax		$ 22,000
Federal Income Tax		4,000
Net Income		$ 18,000

Statement of Changes to Retained Earnings

Earned Surplus, Dec. 31 (previous year)	$73,000	
Preferred Dividend: $2.00 per share	$ 2,000	
Common Dividend: $1.50 per share	$ 9,000	$ 11,000
Balance Carried To Earned Surplus		7,000
Previous Surplus, Dec. 31 (previous year)		$ 73,000
Earned Surplus, December 31 (current year)		$ 80,000

Again referring back to ABC Co., the current ratio would be:

$$\frac{\text{Current Assets}}{\text{Current Liabilities}} \quad = \quad \frac{\$95,000}{\$30,000} \quad = 3.16 \text{ or } 3.16{:}1$$

In the financial industry, the ratio would not be reported as just 3.16, but rather as 3.16 to 1, or 3.16:1. This is telling us that the current assets of ABC Co. cover the current liabilities by 3.16 times as much. Because this analysis is a ratio, it would be reported as 3.16:1. In order to further understand this ratio, lets review it in a somewhat personal manner. Assume you were deciding which one of your friends you were going to invest in or lend money to:

Friend number 1 had $2,000 in bills and $5,000 in the bank.
Friend number 2 had $3,000 in bills and $3,000 in the bank.
Friend number 3 had $10,000 in bills and $6,000 in the bank.
With which friend would you feel most comfortable, other things being equal, making an investment? Probably friend number one.

Current Ratio's = Friend # 1 = 2.5:1
                    = Friend # 2 = 1:1
                    = Friend # 3 = -.6:1

This is very similar to how the financial analyst uses the current ratio in analyzing and comparing corporate liquidity.

As you might have guessed, there is a ratio which analyzes liquidity on an even more stringent level. This test

ABC CORPORATION
BALANCE SHEET   EXHIBIT 1

Current Assets:			Current Liabilities:	
Cash	$25,000		Accounts Payable	$15,000
Accounts Receivable	18,000		Bank Loan	12,000
Inventory	35,000		Accrued Expense	3,000
Securities	17,000		**Total Current Liabilities**	$30,000
Total Current Assets	$95,000			
			Mortgage Bond	110,000
			Total Liabilities	$140,000

Fixed Assets:			Capital and Surplus:	
Plant & Equip.	$300,000		Capital Stock	
Less: Depreciation	85,000		Preferred Stock, 5% ($25 Par)	
Net Property	215,000		1,000 shares outstanding	$25,000
Land	65,000		Common Stock, ($20 Par)	
Goodwill	20,000		6,000 shares outstanding	$120,000
Total Assets	$395,000		Surplus:	
			Capital	$30,000
			Earned	$80,000
Market Price: $40.00 per share			**Total Stockholders Equity**	$255,000

INCOME STATEMENT   EXHIBIT 2

Net Sales:		$150,000
Cost and Expenses		
Cost of Good Sold	$70,000	
Selling Expense	$15,000	
Depreciation	$10,000	
Maintenance	$20,000	
Property Taxes	$ 5,000	$120,000
Operating Profit:		30,000
Interest:		8,000
Income Before Federal Income Tax		$ 22,000
Federal Income Tax		4,000
Net Income		$ 18,000

Statement of Changes to Retained Earnings

Earned Surplus, Dec. 31 (previous year)	$73,000	
Preferred Dividend: $2.00 per share	$ 2,000	
Common Dividend: $1.50 per share	$ 9,000	$ 11,000
Balance Carried To Earned Surplus		7,000
Previous Surplus, Dec. 31 (previous year)		$ 73,000
Earned Surplus, December 31 (current year)		$ 80,000

is called the "**Acid Test**" or "**Quick Ratio**." In using this ratio, as the name implies, we can only use assets which can be converted into cash **quickly**. In viewing our ABC Co. current assets, which item might not be able to be converted quickly into cash? That's right, inventory. Therefore, in computing the "acid test" we simply subtract inventory from our current assets, then use the same formula as in our current ratio. It is as follows:

$$\frac{\text{Current Assets - Inventory}}{\text{Current Liabilities}} \quad = \quad \frac{\$95,000 - \$35,000}{\$30,000} \quad = 2.0\!:\!1$$

ABC CORPORATION
BALANCE SHEET   EXHIBIT 1

Current Assets:			Current Liabilities:	
Cash	$25,000		Accounts Payable	$15,000
Accounts Receivable	18,000		Bank Loan	12,000
Inventory	35,000		Accrued Expense	3,000
Securities	17,000		**Total Current Liabilities**	$30,000
Total Current Assets	$95,000			
			Mortgage Bond	110,000
			Total Liabilities	$140,000

Fixed Assets:			Capital and Surplus:	
Plant & Equip.	$300,000		Capital Stock	
Less: Depreciation	85,000		Preferred Stock, 5% ($25 Par)	
Net Property	215,000		1,000 shares outstanding	$25,000
Land	65,000		Common Stock, ($20 Par)	
Goodwill	20,000		6,000 shares outstanding	$120,000
Total Assets	$395,000		Surplus:	
			Capital	$30,000
			Earned	$80,000
Market Price: $40.00 per share			**Total Stockholders Equity**	$255,000

INCOME STATEMENT   EXHIBIT 2

Net Sales:		$150,000
Cost and Expenses		
Cost of Good Sold	$70,000	
Selling Expense	$15,000	
Depreciation	$10,000	
Maintenance	$20,000	
Property Taxes	$ 5,000	$120,000
Operating Profit:		30,000
Interest:		8,000
Income Before Federal Income Tax		$ 22,000
Federal Income Tax		4,000
Net Income		$ 18,000

Statement of Changes to Retained Earnings

Earned Surplus, Dec. 31 (previous year)	$73,000	
Preferred Dividend: $2.00 per share	$ 2,000	
Common Dividend: $1.50 per share	$ 9,000	$ 11,000
Balance Carried To Earned Surplus		7,000
Previous Surplus, Dec. 31 (previous year)		$ 73,000
Earned Surplus, December 31 (current year)		$ 80,000

Again, using the figures from our ABC Co. (exhibit 1), we compute the "acid test" or "quick ratio" to be 2:1.

Reviewing, our current ratio for ABC Co. is 3.16:1. Most analysts consider a current ratio, for a manufacturing company, of 2:1 to be acceptable. Our quick ratio, is 2:1. Again, most analysts consider a quick ratio of 1:1 to be acceptable. It appears, at least initially, that our company is performing well. However, we cannot be sure until we have calculated the current and quick ratios for other firms in our industry and made subsequent comparisons. This is the only way to know whether our company is performing better than, equal to, or worse than its competitors. These financial comparisons must be made for all ratio's to derive a true and accurate indication of financial performance and wellbeing.

Book Value

The last balance sheet item which we will review is the **"Book Value Per Common Share."** Most of you have heard of the term "book value" before and probably wondered what exactly was being stated.

Book Value simply states the value of a company after all assets are liquidated and liabilities paid. Taking it one step further, book value per common share would be derived by dividing book value by common shares outstanding. Remember, since we are assuming the liquidation of assets, we can only be reasonably sure what we will receive for **"tangible"** assets. Intangible assets could vary widely in their disposal; from absolutely nothing to infinity. Because of this potentially wide variation, intangible assets are excluded from the "book value" calculation.

Book value is important because analysts and investors sometimes like to know, if a company were liquidated,

ABC CORPORATION
BALANCE SHEET   EXHIBIT 1

Current Assets:

Cash	$25,000	
Accounts Receivable	18,000	
Inventory	35,000	
Securities	17,000	
Total Current Assets	$95,000	

Current Liabilities:

Accounts Payable	$15,000
Bank Loan	12,000
Accrued Expense	3,000
Total Current Liabilities	$30,000
Mortgage Bond	110,000
Total Liabilities	$140,000

Fixed Assets:

Plant & Equip.	$300,000	
Less: Depreciation	85,000	
Net Property		215,000
Land		65,000
Goodwill		20,000
Total Assets		$395,000

Capital and Surplus:

Capital Stock	
Preferred Stock, 5% ($25 Par)	
1,000 shares outstanding	$25,000
Common Stock, ($20 Par)	
6,000 shares outstanding	$120,000
Surplus:	
Capital	$30,000
Earned	$80,000
Total Stockholders Equity	$255,000

Market Price: $40.00 per share

INCOME STATEMENT   EXHIBIT 2

Net Sales:		$150,000
Cost and Expenses		
Cost of Good Sold	$70,000	
Selling Expense	$15,000	
Depreciation	$10,000	
Maintenance	$20,000	
Property Taxes	$ 5,000	$120,000
Operating Profit:		30,000
Interest:		8,000
Income Before Federal Income Tax		$ 22,000
Federal Income Tax		4,000
Net Income		$ 18,000

Statement of Changes to Retained Earnings

Earned Surplus, Dec. 31 (previous year)	$73,000	
Preferred Dividend: $2.00 per share	$ 2,000	
Common Dividend: $1.50 per share	$ 9,000	$ 11,000
Balance Carried To Earned Surplus		7,000
Previous Surplus, Dec. 31 (previous year)		$ 73,000
Earned Surplus, December 31 (current year)		$ 80,000

what asset value would be available to pay to common shareholders. Also, when comparing book value per common share to other companies in the same or similar industries, it can be used to indicate whether the company's stock is overbought (high), oversold (low) or fairly valued.

Book value is sometimes referred to as "Net Tangible Asset Value," and book value per common share is similarly called "net tangible asset value per common share". Please do not let the longer name scare you. These two terms are one in the same and are interchangeable. Now that you know what book value per common share is, let's learn the formula and how to calculate it.

ABC CORPORATION
BALANCE SHEET   EXHIBIT 1

Current Assets:		Current Liabilities:	
Cash	$25,000	Accounts Payable	$15,000
Accounts Receivable	18,000	Bank Loan	12,000
Inventory	35,000	Accrued Expense	3,000
Securities	17,000	**Total Current Liabilities**	$30,000
Total Current Assets	$95,000		
		Mortgage Bond	110,000
		Total Liabilities	$140,000

Fixed Assets:			Capital and Surplus:	
Plant & Equip.	$300,000		Capital Stock	
Less: Depreciation	85,000		Preferred Stock, 5% ($25 Par)	
Net Property		215,000	1,000 shares outstanding	$25,000
Land		65,000	Common Stock, ($20 Par)	
Goodwill		20,000	6,000 shares outstanding	$120,000
Total Assets		$395,000	Surplus:	
			Capital	$30,000
			Earned	$80,000
Market Price: $40.00 per share			**Total Stockholders Equity**	$255,000

INCOME STATEMENT   EXHIBIT 2

Net Sales:		$150,000
Cost and Expenses		
Cost of Good Sold	$70,000	
Selling Expense	$15,000	
Depreciation	$10,000	
Maintenance	$20,000	
Property Taxes	$ 5,000	$120,000
Operating Profit:		30,000
Interest:		8,000
Income Before Federal Income Tax		$ 22,000
Federal Income Tax		4,000
Net Income		$ 18,000

Statement of Changes to Retained Earnings

Earned Surplus, Dec. 31 (previous year)	$73,000	
Preferred Dividend: $2.00 per share	$ 2,000	
Common Dividend: $1.50 per share	$ 9,000	$ 11,000
Balance Carried To Earned Surplus		7,000
Previous Surplus, Dec. 31 (previous year)		$ 73,000
Earned Surplus, December 31 (current year)		$ 80,000

Book Value Per Common Share

The formula for Book Value Per Common Share is:

$$\frac{\text{Common Equity - Intangibles}}{\text{\# of Common Shares Outstanding}} = \text{Book Value PCS}$$

Again referring to our ABC Co.:

What is common equity? It is the total stockholders equity less any preferred stockholder equity.

Total stockholder equity - preferred equity = Common Equity
$255,000   - $25,000   = $230,000

What are our intangible assets? Looking at our ABC Co. balance sheet, we see that the only intangible is goodwill, in the amount of $20,000. Now we have sufficient information to complete the book value calculation.

$$\frac{\$230,000 - \$20,000}{6,000} = \frac{\$210,000}{6,000} = \$35.00 \text{ Book Value Per Common Share}$$

If the actual price of ABC's common stock in the marketplace was $45, some might say that the stock was overvalued or overbought. If the price was $25 per share, some might say that the stock was undervalued or oversold. Both suggestions could be right or wrong. The best method to ascertain whether or not the stock is under or over valued, would be, as stated earlier, to compare ABC's book value per common share with other firms in the same or similar industry.

This completes our look at financial ratio's derived from the balance sheet. However, it should be noted that this review is by no means an exhaustive one. As you might imagine, financial analysts have discovered and invented many types of ratio analysis and variations on those

ABC CORPORATION
BALANCE SHEET   EXHIBIT 1

Current Assets:			Current Liabilities:	
Cash	$25,000		Accounts Payable	$15,000
Accounts Receivable	18,000		Bank Loan	12,000
Inventory	35,000		Accrued Expense	3,000
Securities	17,000		**Total Current Liabilities**	$30,000
Total Current Assets	$95,000			
			Mortgage Bond	110,000
			Total Liabilities	$140,000

Fixed Assets:			Capital and Surplus:	
Plant & Equip.	$300,000		Capital Stock	
Less: Depreciation	85,000		Preferred Stock, 5% ($25 Par)	
Net Property		215,000	1,000 shares outstanding	$25,000
Land		65,000	Common Stock, ($20 Par)	
Goodwill		20,000	6,000 shares outstanding	$120,000
Total Assets		$395,000	Surplus:	
			Capital	$30,000
			Earned	$80,000
Market Price: $40.00 per share			**Total Stockholders Equity**	$255,000

INCOME STATEMENT   EXHIBIT 2

Net Sales:		$150,000
Cost and Expenses		
Cost of Good Sold	$70,000	
Selling Expense	$15,000	
Depreciation	$10,000	
Maintenance	$20,000	
Property Taxes	$ 5,000	$120,000
Operating Profit:		30,000
Interest:		8,000
Income Before Federal Income Tax		$ 22,000
Federal Income Tax		4,000
Net Income		$ 18,000

Statement of Changes to Retained Earnings

Earned Surplus, Dec. 31 (previous year)	$73,000	
Preferred Dividend: $2.00 per share	$ 2,000	
Common Dividend: $1.50 per share	$ 9,000	$ 11,000
Balance Carried To Earned Surplus		7,000
Previous Surplus, Dec. 31 (previous year)		$ 73,000
Earned Surplus, December 31 (current year)		$ 80,000

ratio analysis. Those covered above are sufficient for a general understanding of balance sheet ratios.

Let us move on to **income statement** analysis.

ABC CORPORATION
BALANCE SHEET   EXHIBIT 1

Current Assets:

Cash	$25,000
Accounts Receivable	18,000
Inventory	35,000
Securities	17,000
Total Current Assets	$95,000

Fixed Assets:

Plant & Equip.	$300,000	
Less: Depreciation	85,000	
Net Property		215,000
Land		65,000
Goodwill		20,000
Total Assets		$395,000

Market Price: $40.00 per share

Current Liabilities:

Accounts Payable	$15,000
Bank Loan	12,000
Accrued Expense	3,000
Total Current Liabilities	$30,000
Mortgage Bond	110,000
Total Liabilities	$140,000

Capital and Surplus:

Capital Stock	
Preferred Stock, 5% ($25 Par)	
1,000 shares outstanding	$25,000
Common Stock, ($20 Par)	
6,000 shares outstanding	$120,000
Surplus:	
Capital	$30,000
Earned	$80,000
Total Stockholders Equity	$255,000

INCOME STATEMENT   EXHIBIT 2

Net Sales:		$150,000
Cost and Expenses		
Cost of Good Sold	$70,000	
Selling Expense	$15,000	
Depreciation	$10,000	
Maintenance	$20,000	
Property Taxes	$ 5,000	$120,000
Operating Profit:		30,000
Interest:		8,000
Income Before Federal Income Tax		$ 22,000
Federal Income Tax		4,000
Net Income		$ 18,000

Statement of Changes to Retained Earnings

Earned Surplus, Dec. 31 (previous year)	$73,000	
Preferred Dividend: $2.00 per share	$ 2,000	
Common Dividend: $1.50 per share	$ 9,000	$ 11,000
Balance Carried To Earned Surplus		7,000
Previous Surplus, Dec. 31 (previous year)		$ 73,000
Earned Surplus, December 31 (current year)		$ 80,000

INCOME STATEMENT

The **income statement** is the document which states, in detail, all sources of revenue and expenses for a specified period of time. Generally, corporations issue financial statements quarterly (referred to as 10 Q's) and annually (referred to as annual statements or 10 K's).

There is one other part of the income statement, which at times, is considered totally separate and a statement of its own. This is the **"Statement of Changes to Retained Earnings."** This statement is a kind of "go between." It links the income statement to the balance sheet. For the purposes of this text, we will consider it a part of the income statement.

Let's now review the income statement portion of ABC Co.'s financial statements found in exhibit 2.

ABC CORPORATION
BALANCE SHEET   EXHIBIT 1

Current Assets:			Current Liabilities:	
Cash	$25,000		Accounts Payable	$15,000
Accounts Receivable	18,000		Bank Loan	12,000
Inventory	35,000		Accrued Expense	3,000
Securities	17,000		**Total Current Liabilities**	$30,000
Total Current Assets	$95,000			
			Mortgage Bond	110,000
			Total Liabilities	$140,000

Fixed Assets:			Capital and Surplus:	
Plant & Equip.	$300,000		Capital Stock	
Less: Depreciation	85,000		Preferred Stock, 5% ($25 Par)	
Net Property		215,000	1,000 shares outstanding	$25,000
Land		65,000	Common Stock, ($20 Par)	
Goodwill		20,000	6,000 shares outstanding	$120,000
Total Assets		$395,000	Surplus:	
			Capital	$30,000
			Earned	$80,000
Market Price: $40.00 per share			**Total Stockholders Equity**	$255,000

INCOME STATEMENT   EXHIBIT 2

Net Sales:		$150,000
Cost and Expenses		
Cost of Good Sold	$70,000	
Selling Expense	$15,000	
Depreciation	$10,000	
Maintenance	$20,000	
Property Taxes	$ 5,000	$120,000
Operating Profit:		30,000
Interest:		8,000
Income Before Federal Income Tax		$ 22,000
Federal Income Tax		4,000
Net Income		$ 18,000

Statement of Changes to Retained Earnings

Earned Surplus, Dec. 31 (previous year)	$73,000	
Preferred Dividend: $2.00 per share	$ 2,000	
Common Dividend: $1.50 per share	$ 9,000	$ 11,000
Balance Carried To Earned Surplus		7,000
Previous Surplus, Dec. 31 (previous year)		$ 73,000
Earned Surplus, December 31 (current year)		$ 80,000

Net Sales
On some, or most income statements there will be an entry termed "gross sales." From this figure, accountants will subtract out returns and other discounts, thus arriving at net sales. In our example, we have simplified matters.

Cost of Goods Sold
Cost of goods sold is just simply how much is cost the the company to produce the goods or services it sold. Of course there are many different cost associated with doing business and it is here these cost are itemized.

Operating Profit
Operating profit is also interchangeably referred to as "**Operating Margin**." Operating margin is calculated by taking the net sales and subtracting out the cost of goods sold, including the operating expenses.

Interest Expense
Any interest which the company has paid during this current reporting period will be reported and charged against current income.

Income Before Federal Income Tax
This is exactly what it appears to be. Income before Uncle Sam takes his share. On most income statements, "Earnings Before Taxes" will be abbreviated as "EBT." Remember, income is what the corporation has earned. Therefore, income for a corporation after expenses is usually referred to as **earnings**.

Federal Income Tax
Federal income tax is usually the last expense item on the income statement. As you can calculate from exhibit 2, ABC Co. only paid about 18% in taxes (wouldn't it be nice if all income tax rates were this low.)

ABC CORPORATION
BALANCE SHEET   EXHIBIT 1

Current Assets:			Current Liabilities:	
Cash	$25,000		Accounts Payable	$15,000
Accounts Receivable	18,000		Bank Loan	12,000
Inventory	35,000		Accrued Expense	3,000
Securities	17,000		**Total Current Liabilities**	$30,000
Total Current Assets	$95,000			
			Mortgage Bond	110,000
			Total Liabilities	$140,000

Fixed Assets:			Capital and Surplus:	
Plant & Equip.	$300,000		Capital Stock	
Less: Depreciation	85,000		Preferred Stock, 5% ($25 Par)	
Net Property	215,000		1,000 shares outstanding	$25,000
Land	65,000		Common Stock, ($20 Par)	
Goodwill	20,000		6,000 shares outstanding	$120,000
Total Assets	$395,000		Surplus:	
			Capital	$30,000
			Earned	$80,000
Market Price: $40.00 per share			**Total Stockholders Equity**	$255,000

INCOME STATEMENT   EXHIBIT 2

Net Sales:		$150,000
Cost and Expenses		
Cost of Good Sold	$70,000	
Selling Expense	$15,000	
Depreciation	$10,000	
Maintenance	$20,000	
Property Taxes	$ 5,000	$120,000
Operating Profit:		30,000
Interest:		8,000
Income Before Federal Income Tax		$ 22,000
Federal Income Tax		4,000
Net Income		$ 18,000

Statement of Changes to Retained Earnings

Earned Surplus, Dec. 31 (previous year)	$73,000	
Preferred Dividend: $2.00 per share	$ 2,000	
Common Dividend: $1.50 per share	$ 9,000	$ 11,000
Balance Carried To Earned Surplus		7,000
Previous Surplus, Dec. 31 (previous year)		$ 73,000
Earned Surplus, December 31 (current year)		$ 80,000

Net Income   Lastly, we arrive at our company's "Net Income." This is **real money**. This is usually where all dividends, preferred and common, will be paid. Therefore, if this figure is low or even negative, there probably will not be a common stock dividend for this reporting period. Remember, "**net income**" is synonymous with "**net earnings**."

Now let's review the last part of our income statement, the "**Statement of Changes to Retained Earnings**."

Dividend Accounting   As previously mentioned, this section basically "links" the income statement to the balance sheet. Once we have our net income, we must account for dividend payment. After dividend payment, any remaining funds are termed "**retained earnings**" or "**earned surplus**."

Balance Sheet Linkage   Since we have now completed all accounting for our company's income, what do we do with what is remaining? The income statement is just that, a statement of money coming into the corporation, and money flowing out of the corporation. The income statement is not, however, a savings account. We do not store or "save" cash or any other asset on the income statement. Where do we store the assets of our corporation? The balance sheet.

Where do we store the assets of our corporation? The balance sheet.

ABC CORPORATION
BALANCE SHEET   EXHIBIT 1

Current Assets:			Current Liabilities:	
Cash	$25,000		Accounts Payable	$15,000
Accounts Receivable	18,000		Bank Loan	12,000
Inventory	35,000		Accrued Expense	3,000
Securities	17,000		**Total Current Liabilities**	$30,000
Total Current Assets	$95,000			
			Mortgage Bond	110,000
			Total Liabilities	$140,000

Fixed Assets:			Capital and Surplus:	
Plant & Equip.	$300,000		Capital Stock	
Less: Depreciation	85,000		Preferred Stock, 5% ($25 Par)	
Net Property	215,000		1,000 shares outstanding	$25,000
Land	65,000		Common Stock, ($20 Par)	
Goodwill	20,000		6,000 shares outstanding	$120,000
Total Assets	$395,000		Surplus:	
			Capital	$30,000
			Earned	$80,000
Market Price: $40.00 per share			**Total Stockholders Equity**	$255,000

INCOME STATEMENT   EXHIBIT 2

Net Sales:		$150,000
Cost and Expenses		
Cost of Good Sold	$70,000	
Selling Expense	$15,000	
Depreciation	$10,000	
Maintenance	$20,000	
Property Taxes	$ 5,000	$120,000
Operating Profit:		30,000
Interest:		8,000
Income Before Federal Income Tax		$ 22,000
Federal Income Tax		4,000
Net Income		$ 18,000

Statement of Changes to Retained Earnings

Earned Surplus, Dec. 31 (previous year)	$73,000	
Preferred Dividend: $2.00 per share	$ 2,000	
Common Dividend: $1.50 per share	$ 9,000	$ 11,000
Balance Carried To Earned Surplus		7,000
Previous Surplus, Dec. 31 (previous year)		$ 73,000
Earned Surplus, December 31 (current year)		$ 80,000

Balance Sheet Linkage Cont. Therefore, since we have cash remaining after all expenses have been paid, we must have some mechanism available to allow for the **transfer** of this cash from our income statement to our "**savings account**" which is located on the balance sheet. The mechanism afforded to accomplish this task is the "**Statement of Changes to Retained Earnings**."

Reviewing the statement of changes to retained earning in exhibit 2, we find a number of items. Let's look at each one. First we have "**Beginning of Year Retained Earnings**," also called "**Earned Surplus**." This item is taken from the "Stockholders Equity" portion of the **prior reporting** period's balance sheet. This figure is the total of retained earnings in the corporation at the beginning of its current reporting period. This figure represents a cumulative, running total of all retained earning since the corporation began operations. Simply stated, this figure represents the total amount of cash the corporation has "earned and saved" during its corporate life. Hence the term, "retained earnings."

Let's not lose sight of what we are exploring, namely, the linkage between the Balance Sheet and Income Statement, provided through the Statement of Changes to Retained Earnings. Therefore, please note, the **first item** listed on the Statement of Changes to Retained Earnings comes from the balance sheet, more specifically, the prior reporting periods' balance sheet. **Earned Surplus** is a balance sheet item.

The next items listed is the "**dividend accounting**" for the **current** reporting period. These items are income statement items (are you noticing the linkage now?). From our current net income figure, the corporation deducts the amounts which have been disbursed or "paid

ABC CORPORATION
BALANCE SHEET   EXHIBIT 1

Current Assets:

Cash	$25,000
Accounts Receivable	18,000
Inventory	35,000
Securities	17,000
Total Current Assets	$95,000

Current Liabilities:

Accounts Payable	$15,000
Bank Loan	12,000
Accrued Expense	3,000
Total Current Liabilities	$30,000
Mortgage Bond	110,000
Total Liabilities	$140,000

Fixed Assets:

Plant & Equip.	$300,000	
Less: Depreciation	85,000	
Net Property		215,000
Land		65,000
Goodwill		20,000
Total Assets		$395,000

Capital and Surplus:

Capital Stock	
Preferred Stock, 5% ($25 Par)	
1,000 shares outstanding	$25,000
Common Stock, ($20 Par)	
6,000 shares outstanding	$120,000
Surplus:	
Capital	$30,000
Earned	$80,000
Total Stockholders Equity	$255,000

Market Price: $40.00 per share

INCOME STATEMENT   EXHIBIT 2

Net Sales:		$150,000
Cost and Expenses		
Cost of Good Sold	$70,000	
Selling Expense	$15,000	
Depreciation	$10,000	
Maintenance	$20,000	
Property Taxes	$ 5,000	$120,000
Operating Profit:		30,000
Interest:		8,000
Income Before Federal Income Tax		$ 22,000
Federal Income Tax		4,000
Net Income		$ 18,000

Statement of Changes to Retained Earnings

Earned Surplus, Dec. 31 (previous year)	$73,000	
Preferred Dividend: $2.00 per share	$ 2,000	
Common Dividend: $1.50 per share	$ 9,000	$ 11,000
Balance Carried To Earned Surplus		7,000
Previous Surplus, Dec. 31 (previous year)		$ 73,000
Earned Surplus, December 31 (current year)		$ 80,000

out" in preferred and common dividends. After deducting the dividend payments, the remaining cash is called **"Retained Earnings"** or **"Earned Surplus"** for the current period. This amount is added to the previous year's earned surplus and this new figure is our new cumulative total of retained earning or "earned surplus" for the current reporting period.

ABC CORPORATION
BALANCE SHEET   EXHIBIT 1

Current Assets:			Current Liabilities:	
Cash	$25,000		Accounts Payable	$15,000
Accounts Receivable	18,000		Bank Loan	12,000
Inventory	35,000		Accrued Expense	3,000
Securities	17,000		**Total Current Liabilities**	$30,000
Total Current Assets	$95,000			
			Mortgage Bond	110,000
			Total Liabilities	$140,000

Fixed Assets:			Capital and Surplus:	
Plant & Equip.	$300,000		Capital Stock	
Less: Depreciation	85,000		Preferred Stock, 5% ($25 Par)	
Net Property		215,000	1,000 shares outstanding	$25,000
Land		65,000	Common Stock, ($20 Par)	
Goodwill		20,000	6,000 shares outstanding	$120,000
Total Assets		$395,000	Surplus:	
			Capital	$30,000
			Earned	$80,000
Market Price: $40.00 per share			**Total Stockholders Equity**	$255,000

INCOME STATEMENT   EXHIBIT 2

Net Sales:		$150,000
Cost and Expenses		
Cost of Good Sold	$70,000	
Selling Expense	$15,000	
Depreciation	$10,000	
Maintenance	$20,000	
Property Taxes	$ 5,000	$120,000
Operating Profit:		30,000
Interest:		8,000
Income Before Federal Income Tax		$ 22,000
Federal Income Tax		4,000
Net Income		$ 18,000

Statement of Changes to Retained Earnings

Earned Surplus, Dec. 31 (previous year)	$73,000	
Preferred Dividend: $2.00 per share	$ 2,000	
Common Dividend: $1.50 per share	$ 9,000	$ 11,000
Balance Carried To Earned Surplus		7,000
Previous Surplus, Dec. 31 (previous year)		$ 73,000
Earned Surplus, December 31 (current year)		$ 80,000

Balance Sheet Linkage Cont. Now that we have this **new** "earned surplus" figure, what do we do with it? We return it back to the balance sheet.

Remember this retained earnings figure represents cash left over from the operations of the corporation. Moreover, recalling that we cannot store or save cash on the income statement, (for the purposes of our discussion, the statement of changes to retained earnings is part of the income statement) we must transfer this income or earned surplus to the appropriate "savings" item listed on our financial statements. That item would be the earned surplus portion of the Stockholders Equity section of the balance sheet. Referring to our ABC Co. in exhibit 2, the End of Year Earned Surplus of $80,000 would be transferred to the earned surplus portion of ABC Co.'s balance sheet. Reviewing exhibit 1, we see that this transfer has occurred, and is being reflected properly and accurately.

Now that you have an understanding of the link between the income statement and balance sheet, let us now review some of the income statement ratio calculations that financial analysts use in evaluating and comparing income statement strength of corporations.

INCOME STATEMENT RATIOS AND CALCULATIONS

There are five basic ratios used to measure corporate "profitability" which are derived from the income statement. The ratios are:

1) **Operating Margin of Profit Ratio**
2) **Interest Coverage Ratio**
3) **Net Profit Ratio**
4) **Return On Assets**
5) **Cash Flow**

Let's take a moment and review each.

ABC CORPORATION
BALANCE SHEET   EXHIBIT 1

Current Assets:			Current Liabilities:	
Cash	$25,000		Accounts Payable	$15,000
Accounts Receivable	18,000		Bank Loan	12,000
Inventory	35,000		Accrued Expense	3,000
Securities	17,000		**Total Current Liabilities**	$30,000
Total Current Assets	$95,000			
			Mortgage Bond	110,000
			Total Liabilities	$140,000

Fixed Assets:			Capital and Surplus:	
Plant & Equip.	$300,000		Capital Stock	
Less: Depreciation	85,000		Preferred Stock, 5% ($25 Par)	
Net Property		215,000	1,000 shares outstanding	$25,000
Land		65,000	Common Stock, ($20 Par)	
Goodwill		20,000	6,000 shares outstanding	$120,000
Total Assets		$395,000	Surplus:	
			Capital	$30,000
			Earned	$80,000
Market Price: $40.00 per share			**Total Stockholders Equity**	$255,000

INCOME STATEMENT   EXHIBIT 2

Net Sales:		$150,000
Cost and Expenses		
Cost of Good Sold	$70,000	
Selling Expense	$15,000	
Depreciation	$10,000	
Maintenance	$20,000	
Property Taxes	$ 5,000	$120,000
Operating Profit:		30,000
Interest:		8,000
Income Before Federal Income Tax		$ 22,000
Federal Income Tax		4,000
Net Income		$ 18,000

Statement of Changes to Retained Earnings

Earned Surplus, Dec. 31 (previous year)	$73,000	
Preferred Dividend: $2.00 per share	$ 2,000	
Common Dividend: $1.50 per share	$ 9,000	$ 11,000
Balance Carried To Earned Surplus		7,000
Previous Surplus, Dec. 31 (previous year)		$ 73,000
Earned Surplus, December 31 (current year)		$ 80,000

Operating Margin of Profit Ratio

The operating margin of profit ratio compares operating margin to net sales and is a basic measure of operating profitability and the efficiency of corporate management. The formula and calculation for our ABC Co. follow:

$$\text{Operating Margin of Profit} = \frac{\text{Operating Profit}}{\text{Net Sales}} \quad \frac{\$30,000}{\$150,000} = \textbf{20\%}$$

From operations, ABC Co. is earning 20% on sales. Is this good? As previously stated, the only way to know is to compare ABC's ratios with other corporations in the same or similar industries.

Interest Coverage Ratio

This ratio measures the ability of the corporation to meet its interest expense. The operating income as well as any non-operating income is available for interest payment. In our sample ABC Co.'s income statement, there was no **"non-operating"** income. The formula and calculation follows:

$$\text{Interest Coverage Ratio} = \frac{\text{Total Operating and Non-Operating Income}}{\text{Interest Expense}} = \frac{\$30,000}{\$8,000} = \textbf{3.75 times}$$

Net Profit Ratio

The third ratio measures the final profitability of the company after all expenses are deducted. It is calculated as follows:

$$\text{Net Profit Ratio} = \frac{\text{Net Income After Taxes}}{\text{Net Sales}} = \frac{\$18,000}{\$150,000} = \textbf{12\%}$$

Our ABC Co. earned a net profit of 12% after tax on its net sales.

ABC CORPORATION
BALANCE SHEET   EXHIBIT 1

Current Assets:			Current Liabilities:	
Cash	$25,000		Accounts Payable	$15,000
Accounts Receivable	18,000		Bank Loan	12,000
Inventory	35,000		Accrued Expense	3,000
Securities	17,000		**Total Current Liabilities**	$30,000
Total Current Assets	$95,000			
			Mortgage Bond	110,000
			Total Liabilities	$140,000

Fixed Assets:			Capital and Surplus:	
Plant & Equip.	$300,000		Capital Stock	
Less: Depreciation	85,000		Preferred Stock, 5% ($25 Par)	
Net Property	215,000		1,000 shares outstanding	$25,000
Land	65,000		Common Stock, ($20 Par)	
Goodwill	20,000		6,000 shares outstanding	$120,000
Total Assets	$395,000		Surplus:	
			Capital	$30,000
			Earned	$80,000
Market Price: $40.00 per share			**Total Stockholders Equity**	$255,000

INCOME STATEMENT   EXHIBIT 2

Net Sales:		$150,000
Cost and Expenses		
Cost of Good Sold	$70,000	
Selling Expense	$15,000	
Depreciation	$10,000	
Maintenance	$20,000	
Property Taxes	$ 5,000	$120,000
Operating Profit:		30,000
Interest:		8,000
Income Before Federal Income Tax		$ 22,000
Federal Income Tax		4,000
Net Income		$ 18,000

Statement of Changes to Retained Earnings

Earned Surplus, Dec. 31 (previous year)	$73,000	
Preferred Dividend: $2.00 per share	$ 2,000	
Common Dividend: $1.50 per share	$ 9,000	$ 11,000
Balance Carried To Earned Surplus		7,000
Previous Surplus, Dec. 31 (previous year)		$ 73,000
Earned Surplus, December 31 (current year)		$ 80,000

Return On Assets Ratio   The return on assets ratio, compares the net profit after tax to the total tangible assets used in the business. The formula and calculations follow:

$$\text{Return On Assets Ratio} = \frac{\text{Net Income After Tax}}{\text{Total Tangible Assets}} = \frac{\$18,000}{\$375,000} = 4.8\%$$

Our ABC Co. has a Return On Tangible Assets, also commonly referred to ROA or Return On Assets, of 4.8 percent.

Cash Flow   The last item we will review, which comes solely from the income statement is the "**cash flow**" of the corporation. The cash flow analysis represents how much "cash" is flowing through the company after it has met its financial obligations for the current period. Again, the formula and calculations follow:

$$\text{Cash Flow} = \text{Net Income} + \text{Current Depreciation}$$

$$\text{ABC Co.} = \$18,000 + \$10,000 = \$28,000 \text{ Cash Flow}$$

Why do we add in depreciation? Depreciation is an expense which is charged against earnings, reducing reportable income, and payable taxes. But it is not an actual cash expense. Therefore, since our net income (cash) has been reduced by a non-cash item, we must add this non-cash item back in to obtain the correct cash flow figure.

We have now completed our review of Balance Sheet and Income Statement Ratios. The next, and yes, final part of our Fundamental Analysis section, reviews ratios which are derived by utilizing **both** the income statement and the Statement of Changes to Retained Earnings.

ABC CORPORATION
BALANCE SHEET EXHIBIT 1

Current Assets:

Cash	$25,000
Accounts Receivable	18,000
Inventory	35,000
Securities	17,000
Total Current Assets	$95,000

Current Liabilities:

Accounts Payable	$15,000
Bank Loan	12,000
Accrued Expense	3,000
Total Current Liabilities	$30,000
Mortgage Bond	110,000
Total Liabilities	$140,000

Fixed Assets:

Plant & Equip.	$300,000	
Less: Depreciation	85,000	
Net Property		215,000
Land		65,000
Goodwill		20,000
Total Assets		$395,000

Capital and Surplus:

Capital Stock	
Preferred Stock, 5% ($25 Par)	
1,000 shares outstanding	$25,000
Common Stock, ($20 Par)	
6,000 shares outstanding	$120,000
Surplus:	
Capital	$30,000
Earned	$80,000
Total Stockholders Equity	$255,000

Market Price: $40.00 per share

INCOME STATEMENT EXHIBIT 2

Net Sales:		$150,000
Cost and Expenses		
Cost of Good Sold	$70,000	
Selling Expense	$15,000	
Depreciation	$10,000	
Maintenance	$20,000	
Property Taxes	$ 5,000	$120,000
Operating Profit:		30,000
Interest:		8,000
Income Before Federal Income Tax		$ 22,000
Federal Income Tax		4,000
Net Income		$ 18,000

Statement of Changes to Retained Earnings

Earned Surplus, Dec. 31 (previous year)	$73,000	
Preferred Dividend: $2.00 per share	$ 2,000	
Common Dividend: $1.50 per share	$ 9,000	$ 11,000
Balance Carried To Earned Surplus		7,000
Previous Surplus, Dec. 31 (previous year)		$ 73,000
Earned Surplus, December 31 (current year)		$ 80,000

While we have, for our purposes, combined the two together as one income statement, it is important to realize that sometimes they are prepared as separate and independent documents.

ABC CORPORATION
BALANCE SHEET   EXHIBIT 1

Current Assets:			**Current Liabilities**:	
Cash	$25,000		Accounts Payable	$15,000
Accounts Receivable	18,000		Bank Loan	12,000
Inventory	35,000		Accrued Expense	3,000
Securities	17,000		**Total Current Liabilities**	$30,000
Total Current Assets	$95,000			
			Mortgage Bond	110,000
			Total Liabilities	$140,000

Fixed Assets:			**Capital and Surplus**:	
Plant & Equip.	$300,000		Capital Stock	
Less: Depreciation	85,000		Preferred Stock, 5% ($25 Par)	
Net Property		215,000	1,000 shares outstanding	$25,000
Land		65,000	Common Stock, ($20 Par)	
Goodwill		20,000	6,000 shares outstanding	$120,000
Total Assets		$395,000	Surplus:	
			Capital	$30,000
			Earned	$80,000
Market Price: $40.00 per share			**Total Stockholders Equity**	$255,000

INCOME STATEMENT   EXHIBIT 2

Net Sales:		$150,000
Cost and Expenses		
Cost of Good Sold	$70,000	
Selling Expense	$15,000	
Depreciation	$10,000	
Maintenance	$20,000	
Property Taxes	$ 5,000	$120,000
Operating Profit:		30,000
Interest:		8,000
Income Before Federal Income Tax		$ 22,000
Federal Income Tax		4,000
Net Income		$ 18,000

Statement of Changes to Retained Earnings

Earned Surplus, Dec. 31 (previous year)	$73,000	
Preferred Dividend: $2.00 per share	$ 2,000	
Common Dividend: $1.50 per share	$ 9,000	$ 11,000
Balance Carried To Earned Surplus		7,000
Previous Surplus, Dec. 31 (previous year)		$ 73,000
Earned Surplus, December 31 (current year)		$ 80,000

Earnings Per Common Share (EPS) Earnings per common share is generally referred to as just "Earnings Per Share" or EPS. EPS is one of the most well-known and widely used of all the fundamental analysis calculations. The formula is:

$$\text{Earning Per Common Share} = \frac{\text{Net Income - Preferred Dividend}}{\text{Common Shares Outstanding}}$$

$$\text{For ABC} = \frac{\$18,000 - \$2,000}{6,000} = \frac{\$16,000}{6,000} = 2.66$$

The EPS for ABC Co. is $2.66. ABC Co. earned $2.66 for every common share currently outstanding.

Price/Earnings Ratio (P/E) Once we know the EPS, we can calculate the Price/Earnings or PE Ratio. It is probably the second most well known and heavily utilized of the ratios. Its formula is as follows:

$$\text{P/E Ratio} = \frac{\text{Current Market Stock Price}}{\text{Earnings Per Share (EPS)}}$$

$$\text{For ABC Co.} \quad \frac{\$40.00}{\$2.66} = 15.04$$

ABC Co. has a Price/Earnings or PE Ratio of 15.04. This could be good, bad, or neutral depending on the prevailing PE ratios of other companies in industry. As a general rule, P/E ratio's are usually higher for "growth" companies, and lower for "mature" companies.

ABC CORPORATION
BALANCE SHEET   EXHIBIT 1

Current Assets:			Current Liabilities:	
Cash	$25,000		Accounts Payable	$15,000
Accounts Receivable	18,000		Bank Loan	12,000
Inventory	35,000		Accrued Expense	3,000
Securities	17,000		**Total Current Liabilities**	$30,000
Total Current Assets	$95,000			
			Mortgage Bond	110,000
			Total Liabilities	$140,000

Fixed Assets:			Capital and Surplus:	
Plant & Equip.	$300,000		Capital Stock	
Less: Depreciation	85,000		Preferred Stock, 5% ($25 Par)	
Net Property	215,000		1,000 shares outstanding	$25,000
Land	65,000		Common Stock, ($20 Par)	
Goodwill	20,000		6,000 shares outstanding	$120,000
Total Assets	$395,000		Surplus:	
			Capital	$30,000
			Earned	$80,000
Market Price: $40.00 per share			**Total Stockholders Equity**	$255,000

INCOME STATEMENT   EXHIBIT 2

Net Sales:		$150,000
Cost and Expenses		
Cost of Good Sold	$70,000	
Selling Expense	$15,000	
Depreciation	$10,000	
Maintenance	$20,000	
Property Taxes	$ 5,000	$120,000
Operating Profit:		30,000
Interest:		8,000
Income Before Federal Income Tax		$ 22,000
Federal Income Tax		4,000
Net Income		$ 18,000

Statement of Changes to Retained Earnings

Earned Surplus, Dec. 31 (previous year)	$73,000	
Preferred Dividend: $2.00 per share	$ 2,000	
Common Dividend: $1.50 per share	$ 9,000	$ 11,000
Balance Carried To Earned Surplus		7,000
Previous Surplus, Dec. 31 (previous year)		$ 73,000
Earned Surplus, December 31 (current year)		$ 80,000

Dividend Payout Ratio

This ratio measures the portion of common earnings that are actually paid out to common shareholders as a dividend. This ratio can actually be calculated by two different formulas. Both formulas are presented below.

$$\text{Dividend Payout Ratio} = \frac{\text{Common Dividends Paid}}{\text{Earnings Per Common}}$$

$$\text{For ABC} \quad \frac{\$\ 9,000}{\$\ 16,000} = 56.3\ \%$$

ABC Co. paid out 56.3 percent of its earnings to common shareholders.

The dividend payout ratio can also be calculated by using the following formula:

$$\text{Dividend Payout Ratio} = \frac{\text{Common Dividends Paid}}{\text{Common Shares Outstanding}}$$

$$= \frac{\$\ 9,000}{6,000} = \$1.50 \text{ per share}$$

This tells us that ABC Co. paid a $1.50 dividend for each common share. However, it does not give us the dividend payout ratio. In order to obtain this figure, we must take this analysis one step further.

$$\text{Dividend Payout Ratio} = \frac{\text{Dividend per Common Share}}{\text{Earnings Per Common Share}}$$

ABC CORPORATION
BALANCE SHEET   EXHIBIT 1

Current Assets:

		Current Liabilities:	
Cash	$25,000	Accounts Payable	$15,000
Accounts Receivable	18,000	Bank Loan	12,000
Inventory	35,000	Accrued Expense	3,000
Securities	17,000	**Total Current Liabilities**	$30,000
Total Current Assets	$95,000		
		Mortgage Bond	110,000
		Total Liabilities	$140,000

Fixed Assets:

			Capital and Surplus:	
Plant & Equip.	$300,000		Capital Stock	
Less: Depreciation	85,000		Preferred Stock, 5% ($25 Par)	
Net Property		215,000	1,000 shares outstanding	$25,000
Land		65,000	Common Stock, ($20 Par)	
Goodwill		20,000	6,000 shares outstanding	$120,000
Total Assets		$395,000	Surplus:	
			Capital	$30,000
			Earned	$80,000
Market Price: $40.00 per share			**Total Stockholders Equity**	$255,000

INCOME STATEMENT   EXHIBIT 2

Net Sales:		$150,000
Cost and Expenses		
Cost of Good Sold	$70,000	
Selling Expense	$15,000	
Depreciation	$10,000	
Maintenance	$20,000	
Property Taxes	$ 5,000	$120,000
Operating Profit:		30,000
Interest:		8,000
Income Before Federal Income Tax		$ 22,000
Federal Income Tax		4,000
Net Income		$ 18,000

Statement of Changes to Retained Earnings

Earned Surplus, Dec. 31 (previous year)	$73,000	
Preferred Dividend: $2.00 per share	$ 2,000	
Common Dividend: $1.50 per share	$ 9,000	$ 11,000
Balance Carried To Earned Surplus		7,000
Previous Surplus, Dec. 31 (previous year)		$ 73,000
Earned Surplus, December 31 (current year)		$ 80,000

$$\text{For ABC Co.} \quad \frac{\$1.50}{\$2.66} = 56.3\,\%$$

As you can see, the results are the same. This completes our section on fundamental analysis. Now we turn our attention to the other school of thought: Technical Analysis.

TECHNICAL ANALYSIS

Technical analysis primarily has to do with the question of "**when**" to buy or sell. In our previous study of fundamental analysis, we were basically attempting to answer the question of "**what**" to buy or sell. As you recall, in order to determine "what" company to buy or sell, we used various ratios to compare similar companies. Technical analysis uses comparisons as well, comparisons of "charts" as as opposed to ratios.

Technical analysts believe that stock prices tend to rise or fall due to certain "**market wide**" forces. These forces include many different factors, including but not limited to the high and low of a stock during a certain period of time, the trading volume, the current trendline, current moving averages, and certain chart patterns, just to name a few. In the pages that follow, we will review and explain all of the above mentioned technical indicators, as well as some not mentioned above.

One final note before we begin our discussion on technical analysis. If you recall the first section in this chapter dealt with the **risks** inherent in securities investments. Moreover, those risk were segregated in two primary categories. They were "**systematic**" and "**unsystematic**" risk. Fundamental and technical analysis are methods designed and used to quantify, predict, and hopefully control these risks. Technical analysis primarily attempts to ascertain and control systematic risk, while fundamental analysis attempts to ascertain and control unsystematic risk.

Now that we have an understanding of the objective of technical analysis and how that objective differs from that of fundamental analysis, we are ready to begin our technical analysis review.

Chartist

Technical analysts are often called "chartists" because they chart stock price movements and use these subsequent patterns in an attempt to "predict" the future direction of stock prices. In addition, technical analysts also use, as mentioned earlier, volume figures and funds available for investing to help them determine the best time to buy or sell.

One last item of interest should be noted with respect to technical analysis charting. Generally speaking, this type of analysis is used to "predict" short-term trends, usually no longer than 4-6 weeks in the future. Active traders are likely to use "charts" to attempt to determine, in the short term, whether it is likely or not that a stocks price will rise or fall. Over the long run charts are not quite as valid. For longer term investment decisions, fundamental analysis is usually the better approach.

We will not try to make everyone a technical analyst "chartist." For the basis of our discussion, it is only important that you realize and understand the basic types of charts which technical analyst use, and the information that is being conveyed by the chart. Let's review the primary chart patterns.

Uptrend

Downtrend

When the price of a stock continues to go higher and higher over a period of time, this stock is said to be in an **uptrend**. Conversely, when the price continues to trade lower on a daily basis, it is said to be in a **downtrend**. The "chart" or "graph" below depicts both a stock uptrend and downtrend.

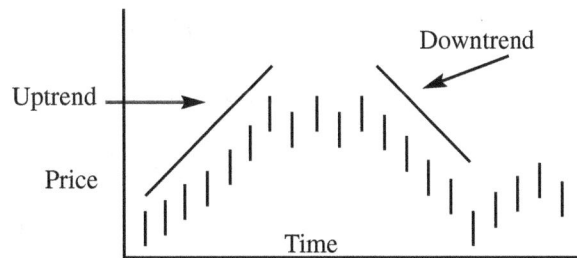

Saucers

If a stock reaches a "high" price above which it does not rise, the stock is said to have reached a "topped" formation or to have "topped out." If a stock reaches a "low" price below which it does not fall below, it is said to have reached a "bottom" formation, or to have "bottomed out."

Saucer formations occur at these so called "topped out" and "bottomed out" levels. A **saucer** formation exist when a stock "bottoms out" and then starts to rise. Conversely, an **inverted saucer** occurs when a stock "tops out" and begins to fall. An example of each is depicted below.

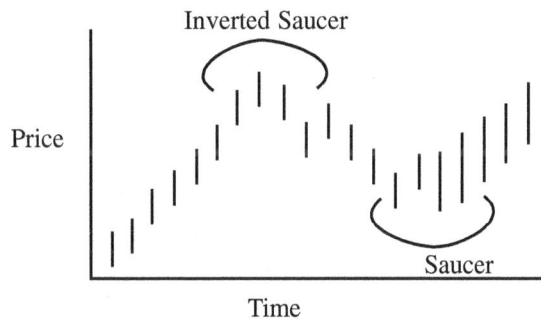

Support and Resistance

If a market continues to test the low of its trading range, but does not break below that level, that particular price point is called "support" or the support level. If the price continues to test the high of its trading range, but does not break above it, that price point is called resistance.

Again, a chart or graph is presented below.

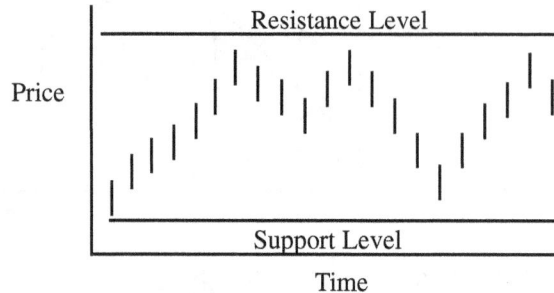

Breakout   When the price movement of a particular security or market "penetrates" or breaks through its established support or resistance levels, that security or market is said to have achieved a "**breakout**." Technicians believe that when a market breaks out through its resistance level, it is a favorable sign and the stock or market should be bought. Conversely, they also believe that when a stock or market breaks out or through its support level, it is a unfavorable sign and should therefore be sold or sold short. A graphical depiction of a breakout is shown below.

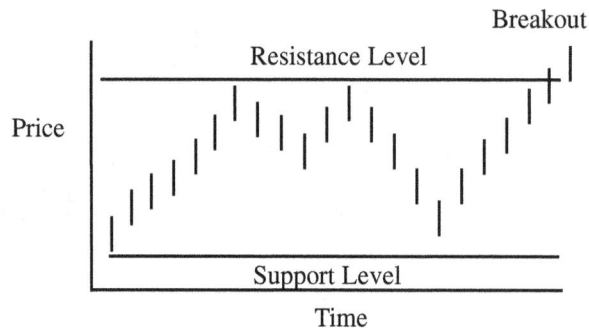

Consolidation If a stock is moving within a narrow range, with no discernable upward or downward pattern, it is said to be moving "sideways." This chart pattern is referred to as a "consolidating" market. Often after a sustained period of rapid price movement, upward or downward, the price appears to pause and just move sideways. Technical analysts theorize this occurs because the "market" is evaluating the current price to determine whether or not it is over, under, or fairly valued. A consolidation chart appears below.

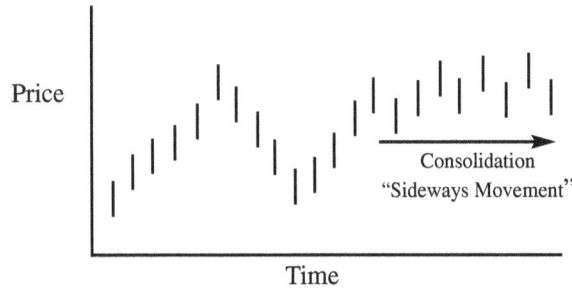

Head and Shoulders

A "head and shoulders" pattern is a type of price pattern formation which, as is indicated by its name, resembles a "head and shoulders" of a human being. This price pattern can occur in two formations. First, it can appear as a normal head and shoulders might appear on a person, this type of formation is called a "**top**" formation. Secondly, it can appear as an inverted or "upside down" pattern. This type of formation is called a "bottom" formation. A chart of a "top" and "bottom" head and shoulders formation is shown below.

Head and Shoulders "Top" Formation

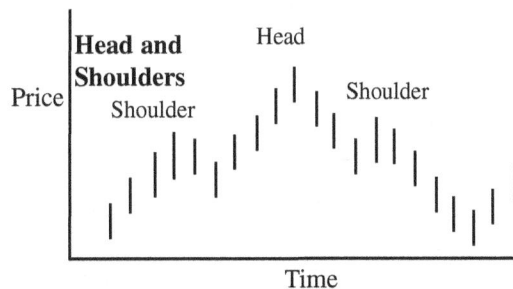

Head and Shoulders "Bottom" Formation

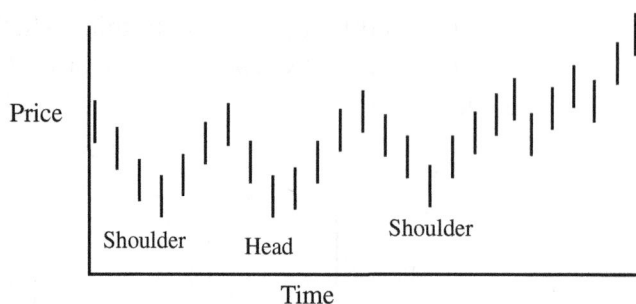

Head and Shoulders Cont.

A head and shoulders "top", indicates that the market has potentially "topped" out and the future trend of prices will be downward. Conversely, a head and shoulders "bottom" indicates the likelihood that a market bottom has been achieved and the future trend of prices will be upward.

Moving Averages

When plotting price points on charts in order to analyze and, hopefully, predict the future trend of market prices, the data may become very erratic and somewhat confusing, thereby causing the analyst to interpret the data, at times, incorrectly. To address this problem, technical analysts have developed many different types of "**smoothing**" applications to apply to a specific chart pattern. While there are many, we will only review the most widely known and used of all "smoothing" techniques, namely the **moving average**.

The moving average is termed such because it is a "rolling" or "moving" sequence of numbers which are also "averaged." Moving averages can be calculated within any specified number of days. For example, assume an investor was using a 50 day moving average. That average would sum all the prices for the past 50 days, and then divide the total by the number of days, which in our example is 50. Therein lies the averaging portion. How is the moving portion of the equation derived? The investor would add the price of the following day, and drop from the averaging calculation, the price from 51 days ago. Each day a new price is added to our calculation, and an old price (51 days old in this example) is deleted. Thus, the average "moves" with market price through time. Hence, the term, moving average. A moving average chart is shown below.

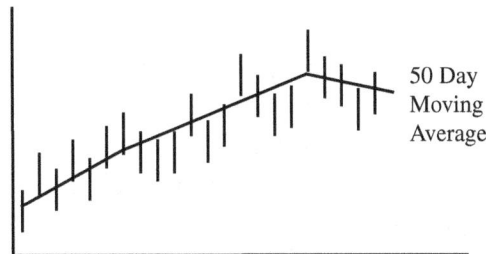

50 Day
Moving
Average

Other Technical Factors and Considerations

Market Strength

Technical analysts use the "strength of the market" to try to ascertain the future direction of prices. One very important indicator of market strength is market volume. If the market is rising on increasing **volume**, technical analysts believe that, near term, prices will continue to rise. However, if the market is rising on decreasing volume, they believe the advance is weakening, and a downturn can be expected. This is sometimes referred to as an **overbought** situation.

Overbought

When a technician says that the market is "**overbought**", he means that after an abundance of buying has occurred, there are few buyers remaining to buy, and therefore a decline in prices can be expected.

Oversold

Conversely, if the market is falling on increasing volume, technicians believe the fall can be expected to accelerate. If however, the market is falling on decreasing volume, technicians believe the fall is weakening and an upturn in prices will soon follow. This falling market with weakening volume is said to be "oversold." An oversold market is one in which there has been so much selling that most investors wishing to sell have already sold. With there being so few sellers now in the market, technicians believe prices will now stabilize and may begin to rise.

Advance/ Decline

Technicians also use a measurement called the analysis to gauge market strength. If the number of issues advancing on the trading day exceeds the number of declining issues, this is said to be a bullish signal. If the number of issues advancing is decreasing, it is said to be a bearish signal. Of course, there are many different types of additional, more complicated advance/decline analyses which technical analysts utilize. For our purposes, to know and understand what the term advance/decline analysis represents will suffice.

Market Momentum

This factor has been defined most appropriately in the sports arena as, the big "**MO**." Just as it is hard to stop the momentum of a sports team on a roll, the same is true of financial markets. Most "momentum" traders will hop on the "big Mo" and hope for a profitable ride!

Available Funds

A major factor in the technical analysis arsenal is the question, "**how much money is available**" to invest? When large institutions, specifically mutual funds, have hordes of cash in their coffers, which at some point in time must be invested, technicians will view this as "bullish." The reason should be obvious. Sooner or later these mutual funds must put this money to work or "invest" in the stock market. After all, the money in their coffers was given to them by individuals with the express purpose of being invested in the market.

Therefore, the mutual fund, pension fund, or other institutional fund manager **must**, at some point, invest this money. When these hordes of purchasing power hit the market, natural laws of supply and demand take over, and stock prices tend to rise.

Conversely, if the large institutional investors are currently close to being fully invested, the demand for stocks will not be as great in the near term and could result in a market decline. Also, if an institution is fully invested and shareholders for some reason decide to redeem part of their holdings, the institution might be placed in the precarious position of having to liquidate stock holdings in order to repay liquidating shareholders. Usually this does not occur because the institution will try to maintain cash a balance sufficient to meet most shareholder redemptions.

As illustrated above, the more "cash" or "funds" available to be invested the better the overall market condition.

Interest Rate Environment

Interest rates are probably the **most** important factor influencing the overall direction of stock prices. The interest rate environment is not only a technical factor, but also a very important factor in fundamental analysis. If you have not already heard one of the most well-known market idioms, let me state it here, "Don't fight the Fed." This saying is simply stating a well-known and well-tested truth, "stock prices overall will tend to **decrease** during an increasing interest rate environment, and **increase** during a decreasing interest rate environment." Why? Technicians believe that as interest rates rise, investors will sell stocks and reinvest in lower risk fixed income securities. Fundamentalist believe that as interest rates rise, the cost of doing business will rise, thus hurting the profitability of the corporate world. The converse is thought to occur in a decreasing interest rate environment.

Indexes

Indexes are also used by technicians to plot and evaluate the movement of overall markets. Technicians believe that by analyzing an index, if they can identify a trend early enough, they can profit from trading securities which mimic or mirror that specific index.

Beta

Beta is the standard measure of risk, for a security, as it relates to the overall market. For instance, the market as a whole has a beta of 1.00, the standard amount of risk. Individual stocks have betas assigned to them by market analyst. A particular stock may have a beta of 1.50, meaning this particular stock has a higher market volatility. Conversely, a stock with a beta of .50 will have about one-half the volatility of the market as a whole.

Conservative issues such as utilities and preferred stocks will have lower betas and high growth issues will tend to have higher betas.

In conclusion, let me reiterate a few main points. First, investing in the stock market or any financial market involves certain risks (Many of those risks were outlined in the opening section of this chapter). Second, there are two primary methods used to analyze and evaluate risk–specifically–fundamental and technical analysis. Fundamental analysis primarily looks at the "company," and the risks associated therein. Technical analysis looks at the company, industry or the market as a whole to asses and evaluate "timing" risk associated with securities investments.

The introduction to securities analysis given in this text is sufficient to provide a basic understanding of securities analysis and the two primary methodologies in practice today. However, for those who have a keen interest and desire to learn more on this subject, libraries and bookstore shelves are loaded with literature on the subject.

Now let us continue by discussing another very influential factor in security price direction. Namely, the overall economic environment.

8

Economics

"...Christmas is a time when kids tell Santa what they want and adults pay for it. Deficits are when adults tell the government what they want–and their kids pay for it..."

Richard Lamm
(1935-   )
Governor of Colorado

ECONOMICS

While fundamental and technical analysts evaluate specific investments and the timing of those investments, they must also concern themselves (as must every investor) with the overall economic condition of their particular marketplace. For instance, would you want to invest in a company that was financially sound and appeared to be perfectly timed for a buy **if** general economic conditions suggested that a broad economic decline, sometimes referred to as a depression, was on the horizon? Probably not. Therefore, all investors, at the very least, need a basic knowledge and understanding of general economics and how it affects overall financial markets.

The Business Cycle

Most occurrences related to nature tend to run in cycles like day and night, the weather, and the seasons to name a few. Therefore, it should not be surprising that man made phenomena, such as the economy, tend to behave cyclically as well.

The **business cycle**, is the pattern of economic behavior which tends to be consistent and repetitive. It has been thusly termed a "**cycle**." There are four recognized phases of the business cycle. They are:

1) Expansion
2) Prosperity
3) Recession
4) Recovery

Expansion

Expansion begins when the economy is at a low point and starts to increase economic activity and real GDP (Gross Domestic Product). After a period of expansion, the economy reaches a peak. This "peak," which can be sustained for quite sometime, is the **prosperity** phase. Eventually the economic climate starts to weaken, and

Prosperity

Recession

Recovery

GDP actually starts to decline. After two successive quarters of GDP decline, the economy has reached the next phase of the cycle, **recession**. Finally, after drudging through the recessionary phase, economic activity increases, and the **recovery** phase begins.

Gross Domestic Product

The primary measure of business activity in the U.S. is Gross Domestic Product (GDP). Gross Domestic Product measures the total of all goods and services produced in the country. The most widely used form of this measure is the "real" GDP. Real GDP is adjusted for the effect of inflation to give the user a more accurate accounting of economic activity.

Factors Influencing the Business Cycle

Fiscal Policy

Fiscal policy is primarily the policies or actions instituted by legislatures to attempt to affect a desired economic outcome. For example, if the U. S. Congress enacts a tax cut, that action would be an exercise of fiscal policy. The government could also decide to cut spending, or increase spending, both of which represent, fiscal policy actions.

Monetary Policy

Monetary policy refers to action taken by the **Federal Reserve Board**. These actions are primarily concerned with affecting or influencing the nation's money supply. The FED has many tools at their disposal, however, the most widely known is their ability to, you guessed it, **raise or lower interest rates**.

Monetary Environment

The term "Monetary Environment" is used to describe the total environment. It looks "holistically" at fiscal **and** monetary policy to determine the "favorableness" or "unfavorableness" of the total monetary environment. For instance, the monetary environment is favorable when government policies are stimulative, interest rates are low; and money supply levels are able to support continued growth. The monetary environment is unfavorable when government policies are restrictive, interest rates are high, and money supply levels are not sufficient to support and sustain incremental growth.

General Economic Theories

Over the decades, there has been a plethora of economic theories put forth to explain the reason for the business cycle. However, only three are considered by most economists to be noteworthy. They are all either fiscal or monetary based.

Keynesian Theory Keynesian Theory was first developed in the early 1930's by economist John Maynard Keynes. He advocated using governmental tools as a means for achieving a stable economic environment of growth. He believed that consumption was the engine of economic activity and that the government was the most viable source for providing the stimulus for consumption.

Monetarist Theory Monetarist theory has no single developer, but rather was developed over time with the contributions of many economists. Monetary theorists believe that monetary policy is the main driving force of economic activity. They argue that the actions of the Federal Reserve Board are primarily responsible for the level of economic activity in the U. S.

Supply Side Theory Supply side theory is similar to Keynesian theory in that both assert the primary role of government in spurring economic activity. However, they do differ. Supply side theorists believe that the government should not institute spending programs, but rather, should use their legislative power to put more money in the hands of consumers, preferably via tax cuts. They further suggest that with this increased disposable income, the consumer will either spend or invest, which will subsequently be reflected in future economic activity.

Supply side theorists argue that instead of the government taking an "**active**" role through spending, it should take a "**passive**" role through tax cuts.

It should be noted that each theory has its supporters and detractors. Now that you are aware of the three predominant economic theories, you will undoubtedly find economic theory debates more interesting.

Economics and Prices

Inflation

Inflation is nothing more than the general increase in price levels relative to economic output. Said another way, if the level of economic output remains constant, and prices rise, the economy is experiencing "**inflation**." Inflation is generally associated with a growing economy. There is a generally recognized theory that the higher the economic growth rate, the greater the eventual likelihood of inflation.

Deflation

Deflation is the opposite of inflation. When economic output is constant, and prices are falling, the economy is experiencing deflation. Deflation represents, as does inflation, a reduction in purchasing power. Deflation can occur for many reasons. However, the usual culprit is mismanagement of fiscal policies resulting in trade deficits, budget deficits, and balance of payments deficits. Deflation usually occurs due to the erosion or devaluation of a country's currency.

Consumer Price Index (CPI)

The consumer price index (CPI) is a basket of "prices" that are combined to arrive at a standard or "indexed" price level. From this established level, prices are measured from month to month and are reported to the general public as up, down, or unchanged from the previous reporting period. Because the number is compared to the previous month, it is a rolling or moving number.

Producer Price Index (PPI)

The producer price index is similar to the CPI as a measurement tool, with the exception of what it measures. While the CPI measures items purchased by consumers, the PPI concentrates on prices of products usually purchased by producing companies. Those items include farm products, industrial commodities, and wages.

Real Interest Rates

All interest rates have a certain amount of risk factored into the current rate. In order to gauge the "**real**" interest rate of a particular security, the investor would subtract the current annual rate of inflation. For example, if a 30-year bond was yielding 6 1/2 %, and the current annual inflation rate was 3%, the "**real**" interest rate would be 3 1/2%.

Functions Of The Federal Reserve

Money Growth

Money growth plays an important role in the economy. Generally, when a country's economy is in a recession, the central bank will take action to increase the money supply. Conversely, when the economy is overheating, the central bank will enact measures to reduce the money supply. In the U.S., the Federal Reserve controls the expansion and contraction of the money supply.

Reserve Requirements

The Federal Reserve is charged with the responsibility of regulating and monitoring the banking industry. A reserve requirement is the percentage of cash reserves the bank **must** keep on deposit with the FED at all times.

Discount Rate   The Fed also, when it deems necessary, adjusts interest rates. While there are several different types of interest rates which can be adjusted, the discount rate has the greatest societal impact. This is because many types of interest bearing loan rates (auto, home equity, margin, credit cards,and prime rate) are tied to the discount rate. If the FED feels the economy needs to be stimulated, it will lower the discount rate. If it wants to restrain the economy, it will increase the discount rate.

Open Market Operations   The FED is able to adjust the cost of credit on a daily basis. This is accomplished by either purchasing or selling certain securities in the marketplace. Because these activities are transacted in the open marketplace, they are said to be "open market operations."

Money Measurement   As mentioned earlier, the FED has the ability to increase or decrease the money supply. In order to accomplish this task, there must be some form of money measurement. They are; **M-1**, **M-2**, and **M-3**.

   M-1 All currency in circulation plus "demand deposits."(checking account money).
   M-2 M-1 plus time deposits (savings accounts, CD's) less than $100,000.
   M-3 The broadest definition of money; M-2 plus time deposits over $100,000.

Business Cycle Indicators

Business indicators are published by the U.S. government on a monthly basis. While there are many different types of indicators, they all fall into 3 distinct categories. They are:

1) Leading Economic Indicators
2) Coincident Economic Indicators
3) Lagging Economic Indicators

Leading economic indicators, as the name suggest, are economic measurements that tend to "**lead**" or show the future course of economic activity. **Coincident indicators**, are economic measurements that economists believe give an indication of the **current** economic climate. Finally, **lagging economic indicators**, again as the name suggests, are economic indicators which "**lag**" the current economic state. In other words, lagging economic indicators give us a lagging picture, or indicate where the economy **has been** over the past month(s). Of the 3 categories, the "leading" indicators are the most widely known and watched. This is because policy makers - such as the FED - use these indicators as input when deciding to raise, lower, or maintain the interest rate environment. A list of the leading, coincident, and lagging indicators is given in exhibit 1.

Consumer Confidence Index

There are two other economic indicators which have been developed in recent years and have gained widespread notoriety and therefore merit mention in this text. The first is the "**Consumer Confidence**" index. This index is somewhat of a "**poll**," which asks consumers are they more or less confident in their economic future. The general idea is that if consumers are more confident relative to the last measure, they will tend to spend more, and economic activity will increase. Conversely, if less confident, they will spend less and economic activity will decrease. The second item is the "**Help Wanted**" index. This indicator measures the volume of "help wanted" advertising in the U.S. and suggests that as economic activity increases so does hiring. A reduction in this index would suggest a contracting economy.

Help Wanted Index

Economic Indicators

Leading	**Coincident**	**Lagging**
New Conusmer Good Orders	Personal Income	Employment Duration
Initial Cliams for Unemployment	Industrial Production	Inventory To Sales Ratio
Length of Manufacturing Workweek	Employment Levels	Labor Cost per Manufactured Unit
Delivery Delays By Vendors	Manufacturing and Trade Sales	Commercial Loans Outstanding
Building Permits	Gross National Products	Ratio of Consumer Credit to Income Level
Contract for Plant and Equipment		Reported Corporate Profit
Change in Manufacturer's Unfilled Durable Goods Orders		
Stock Prices Measured By S& P 500 Average		
Change in Sensitive Materials Prices		
Index of Consumer Expections		
Money Supply Level (M-2)		

Exhibit 1

Economics and Currency Markets

A currency is a country's money. It is the medium used to pay for the purchase of goods and services. Over time, money has become a security tradable in very much the same manner as stocks, bonds, and mutual funds. There are however, some trading distinctions which will be detailed later in this section. As with other securities, there are certain factors which influence the value of a particular country's currency.

For example, the value assigned to a particular stock reflects the current and future success of the company as perceived by the public at a particular point in time. In order to arrive at this value, investors consider many factors, but one could say that the primary consideration is; 'Is the company profitable or unprofitable, and does the company's future prospects look favorable or unfavorable'. These are the same primary considerations involved in valuing currencies; is the country profitable or unprofitable, and does the country's economic future look favorable or unfavorable?

In order to answer this question, we must analyze several economic measurements which indicate the financial health and solvency of a particular country.

Balance of Payments   The "balance of payments" is basically an accounting of our import and export markets and their respective relationship. It seeks to measure whether the country is "making" money (Surplus) or losing money (Deficit). The balance of payments is calculated by taking the value of total exports, and subtracting total imports. (Exports - Imports) If this number is a positive number, **Trade Surplus**   the country is said to have a **trade "surplus"** balance of payments, meaning the country is garnering assets from other countries and redistributing them in their country. This is a favorable economic condition. The country is realizing "profits" from the world. Conversely, if the **Trade Deficit**   number is negative, the country is said to have a **trade**

"**deficit**." This is a negative economic condition because other countries are taking assets out of this country and redistributing those assets to their countrymen. If a country continually runs trade deficits, it will eventually be stripped of its economic capital.

Balance of Payments Cont.

If a country consistently runs a trade surplus, the value of that country's currency, other factors notwithstanding, will rise. This is because the country is becoming richer as a whole, and the standard of value for a country is its currency. Conversely, if trade deficits persist, the country is becoming poorer and might be at risk of going (yes it has happened) bankrupt. As you might expect in this scenario, the country's currency would decline substantially. As an aside, you should be aware that the U.S. has historically (over the last 15-20 yrs) run huge trade deficits.

Credit Worthiness

Another factor that influences currency values, is the ability of a country to pay its creditors. Let's draw a personal analogy. When an individual attempts to borrow money, the financial institution will analyze many factors during the loan approval process. Chief among those factors is whether or not the individual has enough income (financial ability) to service the debt. Basically, can the individual meet the monthly payments? The same is true for a country. When foreign investors buy a governments fixed income securities, they are essentially lending money to that government. They are relying on that government to repay their principle investment plus any accrued interest. If this country is handling its

Budget Surplus

fiscal policy prudently, it will be running **budget surpluses** and amassing "savings" which can be used, if necessary, to repay foreign investors. This will increase foreign confidence in the financial health and stability of a country resulting in an increase in the value of that

Budget Deficit country's currency. Conversely, a consistent **budget deficit**, will tend to make foreign investors skeptical of whether or not their investment or "loan" will be repaid. This skepticism will result in lower rates of foreign investment and will have a negative impact on the currency value. Again it should be noted that the U.S. has traditionally run budget deficits.

Interest Rate Environment The last factor we will review with respect to currency valuation, is the interest rate environment. If interest rates are higher in a particular country, vìs-a-vìs other countries, capital will flow into the country yielding the higher return. This investment capital will stimulate the economy, causing security prices to rise, and currency values to increase. The opposite will occur if interest rates fall below other international rates.

Trading of Currency Markets

Interbank Market Foreign currencies are not traded on any type of exchange, but rather are traded in what is called the "**Interbank Market**." This market is used almost exclusively by professional traders and institutional investors. It is global in scope, very liquid, and open 24 hours a day. Trading is unregulated, primarily due to the professional makeup and globalness of this market. Finally, the trading units are very large, with minimums usually set at $5,000,000.

Spot Market Because trading is unregulated, buyer and seller negotiate their settlement terms. Settlements which are consummated on the first or second business day are referred to as "**spot market**" transactions. Trades which **Forward Contracts** settle later than "spot," are referred to as "**forward contracts**." A forward contract could have a time duration from a few days, to months, to years.

Central Bank Operations

Central banks are very active in the currency markets. If a central bank feels its currency is undervalued, it could buy its own currency in the marketplace and drive the value up. It could sell its currency if it felt the currency was overvalued. This central bank activity in the foreign currency marketplace is called "**intervention**." While central bank intervention is very effective in influencing the **short-term** currency direction, it is much weaker in establishing or maintaining a longer term trend. General economic conditions reviewed earlier in this section, will eventually dictate the currency direction and valuation.

Because trading in the currency markets take place with such large quantities, participants can win or lose vast amounts of money in very short periods of time.

Lastly, you should know that the currency market is the largest financial market in the world. Its size dwarfs that of U.S. stock and bond markets combined. As it currently exists, the currency market is the final frontier for unrestricted and unmitigated financial capital speculation. CAVEAT EMPTOR. (Buyer Beware)

9

Options

"...Take calculated risks. That
is quite different from being
rash..."

George S. Patton
(1885-1945)
General, U.S. Army

OPTIONS

Options!! What are options??? Technically speaking, options are a specific type of security in the family of securities called **"derivatives."** As the family name implies, options are securities which are "derived from" or based upon other underlying securities. Thoroughly confused yet? Let me try to make it a little clearer.

Options have existed in the business world for quite some time. One of the most frequently used options, prior to financial options, was the "option" to purchase real estate. For example, if a real estate investor thought a particular piece of land was going to appreciate for any number of reasons, instead of purchasing the land outright, that investor might attempt to purchase an "option" on the property. That is, the investor would purchase a **"right"** to buy the property by some specified time in the future, and at a predetermined price. The terms of this agreement were drawn up in a legal document, called an "option." Of course to obtain the right to buy this property at some point in the future, the person desiring this right is required to give some type of **"consideration"** to the person granting this right.

"Consideration" is one of the required ingredients of most binding legal contracts. Well, what do you think is the most common type of consideration? You guessed it, MONEY. The person desiring the option pays the person granting the option a certain agreed upon purchase price. Options on securities, work in much the same way. The primary difference is, instead of buyer and seller coming together to negotiate terms, terms are basically standardized, and an intermediary called an options exchange handles the transactions.

Derivative options, and the strategies derived therefrom, have evolved over the last couple of decades to become very complex and difficult to understand, even for professionals in the brokerage industry. For our purposes, however, I will present the basic terminology and concepts of options necessary to give the reader a fundamental awareness and understanding of these types of securities.

Option Terminology

Definition   As with our real estate example, a securities option contract is an agreement between two parties assigning certain rights and obligations to each. When an investor purchases an option they are said to be the "holder." Conversely, when an investor sells an option, they are said to be a "writer" of an option.

Long/Short   When an investor purchases securities, they are said to be "**long**" the security. When an investor has sold or written options, they are said to be "short" the security.

There are two types of options: "**Calls**" and "**Puts**".

Call   A "call" is a type of option which gives the purchaser the right to **buy** 100 shares of a stock at a predetermined price for a specified period of time. It is termed a "call" because it grants the purchaser the right to "call" the stock away from the owner for the predetermined price within the specified period of time.

Put   A "put" is an option which grants the purchaser the right to **sell** 100 shares of a stock to someone else for the predetermined price within the specified period of time. This type of option is termed a "put" option because it gives the holder the right to essentially "put" the stock into another investor hands.

Strike Price   As mentioned earlier, option contracts are fairly standardized, meaning most terms of the contract are uniform. The fixed price specified in the contract at which the holder can either "call away" or "put" the security is called the "**strike price**," or exercise price.

Underlying Security   The underlying security is the actual asset the option is based upon. In our opening example, the underlying security was, real estate. Options are available on most assets and even groups of assets.

Underlying Multiplier   The "purchase unit" of the underlying security represented by the option will vary according to the underlying security itself. In other words, an option for a stock usually covers 100 shares. Whereas an option on other securities, such as bonds, commodities, or currencies, could and do represent completely different standardized "units" of the underlying security.

Expiration Date   As the name implies, this is the actual date after which the option will cease to exist. Obviously, an investor holding options would want to sell or exercise prior to or on this date.

Option strike prices have three pricing categories within which all reside. They are:
1) In-the-Money
2) Out-of-the-money
3) At-the-Money

Let's briefly examine each:

In the Money   An "in-the-money" option is one which its strike price (for a call) is **lower** than the securities' current price. For a "put," the strike price is **higher** than the prevailing market price of the security.

Out of The Money   This situation is the reverse of the in the money situation. A "call" is out of the money when its strike price is **higher** than the underlying's current market price. A "put" is out of the money when its strike price is **lower** than the underlying's current market price.

At the Money Any option, whether put or call, is said to be "at-the-money" when its strike price **is equal to** the current market price.

Option Premiums

Premium The option premium represents the total cost of the option. This premium or "purchase price" has two basic components. They are:

1) Intrinsic Value
2) Time Value

Formula = Intrinsic Value + Time Value = Premium

Let us explore each:

Intrinsic Value Intrinsic value is the amount the option is "in-the-money." For example, assume a stock is currently selling for $50. Also, assume that the investor is considering purchasing a call option with a strike price of 45. Since the option is five points in the money, the option is said to have an intrinsic value of 5 points.

Time Value The time value component is the amount of the purchase price over and above the intrinsic value. Again using our example above, if the purchase price for the 45 strike option is 8, what is the time value? The answer is 3 points. The formula is:

Total Purchase Price - Intrinsic Value = Time Value

The time value portion of the option price will vary according to the duration of time remaining on the option. The more time remaining on the option, the higher the time value portion of the option. If an option is out-of-the-money, then obviously there is no intrinsic value, therefore the total cost of the option represents time value only.

Parity

The last pricing term we will discuss is "parity." Parity refers to the point in time when the option premium equals the intrinsic value. No "time value" is present in the pricing equation.

Option Rules and Regulations

Options Clearing Corporation (OCC)

Options trade in such a fast and furious manner, it is imperative to have some overriding and overseeing entity to regulate and administrate this vast and quick paced market. That entity is the **"Options Clearing Corporation."** It is responsible for randomly assigning exercised options, disseminating information regarding changes in symbols, strike prices, and underlying multipliers. The Options Clearing Corporation is recognized as the definitive, authoritative body and is relied upon by most firms in the brokerage industry.

Options Account Agreement

The "options account agreement" is the document which specifies certain financial and experience information which is critical in assessing the options trading "suitability" of the applicant.

Optional Disclosure Document

Along with the account agreement, the options disclosure document must be supplied to every prospective applicant. This document is a very detailed booklet which explains the options market in general and certain "well known" concepts in particular.

Settlement Date

While stocks settle in three business days, options **settle in one business day**. Because of this one business day settlement, and the risk associated with options, most brokerage firms require the purchaser, or naked seller, to have "cleared" funds in the account at the time of the trade.

Trading Suspension

If you recall from an earlier discussion, options are derivatives. Therefore, if the security from which they are derived ceases to trade, the option will also cease to trade. The trading in that particular option will remain halted until the halt in the underlying security is lifted. However, the investor – irrespective of any trading halt, always retains the right to exercise his or her position. This right is guaranteed by the Options Clearing Corporation (OCC).

Exercise

An exercise is when the option holder decides to implement the right granted under the option contract. Due to the complexities of exercises, they are assigned randomly by a third party organization. That organization is the Options Clearing Corporation.

Automatic Exercise

Generally, in order to exercise an option position, the investor must make a request through the brokerage firm which in turn submits that request to the OCC. However, there were occurrences when the investor did not request an exercise (for any number of reasons) when it was clearly in the investors favor. To address this area of potential conflict, the OCC instituted rules which state that any option which is 1/4 point or more in the money must be automatically exercised unless the investor specifically requests otherwise.

Expiration

All financial options, stocks options or otherwise, expire on the **Saturday after the third Friday** of the expiration month. It is important to note that they do not expire "technically" on the third Saturday, but the Saturday **after** the third Friday of the expiration month.

10

Qualified Plans

"...The question isn't at what
age I want to retire, it's at
what income..."

George Foreman
(1949-   )
American Boxing Champion

QUALIFIED RETIREMENT PLANS

In this day and age, as most are aware, the individual can no longer expect nor rely on the government to provide the means necessary for their financial comfort and security post retirement. If you do not take the time to plan and provide for your own post retirement financial security, trust me, it won't be there. Therefore this section, in my opinion, is one of the most important within this book.

When we think of "retirement plans," we are generally thinking of plans sanctioned and approved by the U.S. Congress, granting specific "**tax related**" benefits to plan participants. These plans are called "**Qualified Retirement Plans**." They have been "qualified" by the U.S. Congress to enjoy special beneficial tax treatment from the Internal Revenue Service. Any retirement plan which does not enjoy this "special tax treatment" is termed "**Unqualified**." In the pages that follow, I will review those types of qualified plans which are most well known and most commonly utilized by the American public.

There are two primary types of qualified retirement plans; those that are "individual" based and those that are "employer" based. We will begin our review with the individual-based plans.

Individual Retirement Accounts (IRAs)

Any Person Employed   Any person currently employed is eligible to open and maintain an IRA account. The individual is allowed to contribute any amount up to a maximum of **$4,000** per year. This contribution is "**deducted**" from the individuals gross income when computing year-end taxable income. Married couples filing "jointly" where both persons work, are allowed to contribute up to $4,000 each to separate IRA accounts, bringing the maximum total for married couples filing jointly to $8000.

Deductibility   The contribution amount is always deductible if the employee is not covered by any other "employer based" retirement or pension plan. If however, the employee is covered by an additional employer based plan, the deductibility of the contribution phases out as the salary level of the employee increases.

> Note: The tax laws are very dynamic, complex and constantly changing. Therefore, one should always consult a tax advisor prior to making any decision with tax implications.

Term of Contributions   Contributions to IRAs are allowed up to the age of 70 1/2.

Contribution Withdrawals   Voluntary withdrawals cannot be made, without penalty, prior to the age of 59 1/2. If a withdrawal is made prior to the participant reaching the age of 59 1/2, the **withdrawal** is subject to normal income tax plus an additional tax penalty of **10** %.

Withdrawals **must**, however, be commenced by April 1 of the year **after** the participant turns 70 1/2. Basically, after you reach the age of about 71, the IRS forces a mandatory partial withdrawal of contributions

Catch-up Provision   The IRS has recently acknowledged the fact that many older American workers do not have sufficient savings to providefor their retirement, and are in need of an immediate tool to help increase their level of savings prior to retirement. To assist in this need, the IRS has eastablished the **"catch-up"** provision, this provision allows persons 50 years or older to save more than persons under 50. For IRA's the extra savings is $1,000.00

Permitted Investments

Because the IRA is a vehicle tailored for "savings" and more specifically for retirement savings, the IRS has established rules which state very clearly what investments are "suitable" and, therefore, "allowable" in an IRA account. Normally, there would be a public outcry if the government attempted to define, direct, or limit the scope of an individual's investment choice but since the government grants special tax privileges for adherence to this policy, and because it generally makes sense, the public has accepted these restrictions.

The "allowed" investments are:

1) Stocks
2) Bonds
3) Unit Trust
4) Mutual Funds
5) Govt. Securities

6) Annuities
7) Gold & Silver Coins minted by the U.S. Treasury.
8) Selling Covered Calls Purchasing Puts

The "disallowed" investments are:

1) Cash Value Insurance Policies
2) Term Insurance
3) Art and Collectibles

These lists may not be exhaustive due to the dynamic nature of tax law, and some items listed may fluctuate on or off the list periodically. However, the salient point is to know that all investments are not allowed in retirement accounts. Generally, those excluded tend to be more risky and more speculative, adding an inordinate amount of risk to an account designed to provide financial safety and securityfor post retirement life.

Custodian Funds invested in an IRA can be moved between "Custodians." A custodian is nothing more than the company holding your IRA account. Not every company can be a custodian. Custodians have to meet certain IRS requirements and must apply for and be granted approval before it can act as an IRA custodian on behalf of investors. The process could be long and arduous, with no guarantee of ever receiving IRS approval.

There are two methods available to IRA account holders for switching between custodians. IRA Rollovers and IRA Transfers. We briefly review each below.

IRA Rollover The "rollover" is probably the most misunderstood of the two. I will attempt to make this explanation as clear and concise as possible. The IRS allows the IRA account holder to "take possession" of the IRA money and do whatever the person wishes to do with the money, as long as the funds are **redeposited** in another "**qualified**" plan within 60 days of the distribution date. The IRS allows this type of non-penalty withdrawal **once** per year. If the funds are not redeposited within the 60 day period, the withdrawal is treated as a "premature withdrawal" with applicable taxes and penalties. The salient point to remember is that the IRA holder is only allowed to "**take possession**" of the funds **once** per year, and they must be **redeposited** within **60 days** of the distribution date.

IRA Transfer IRA Transfers, on the other hand, **do not** pass through (technically speaking) the IRA account holders hands. This type of IRA asset transfer occurs **directly** between the **custodial** organizations. There is no limit on the number of "direct transfers" which can be affected each year. The point of emphasis for determining whether or not a transfer is a "Rollover" or a "Direct Transfer" is how the check is made out. If a check is disbursed from an IRA made out to the individual only, it is considered a "rollover." If the disbursement check is made out to another institution, **for the benefit** of the IRA account holder, the disbursement is considered a "transfer."

Notice that the primary point of interest for the IRS is not **where** the disbursement is mailed, or **who** receives the disbursement, but rather **how** the disbursement check is made out.

If the transfer is effected directly between the custodial organizations via electronic means, then obviously, it would be considered, for tax purposes, a direct transfer.

Roth IRA

The Roth IRA is similar to a regular IRA with a few notable distinctions. The Roth IRA is fairly new, beginning its existence as of January 1, 1998. The differences between regular IRA's and Roth IRA's are listed below. However, qualified retirement plans, particularly new plans, should be thoroughly investigated with the assistance of qualified advisors.

Contributions Contributions are made with **after-tax dollars**. **This distinction is the most major difference between traditional and Roth IRAs**. Because contributions are made with after-tax dollars, withdrawal of principal is made without incurring any tax or IRS penalty.

Also, contributions grow tax deferred. If there are no withdrawals for at least 5 years, the earnings also become tax-free. This is a significant departure from the taxation rules of traditional IRAs. After this 5 year period, funds may be removed tax-free after any of the following occur.

1) attain age 59 1/2
2) Disability
3) first home purchase
4) death

Individuals may contribute up to $4,000 per year if their adjusted gross income is less than $95,000. If an individual's adjusted gross income is over $160,000, no contribution is allowed. Married couples filing jointly may contribute $8,000 ($4,000 each) if their adjusted gross income is $150,000 or less. These contribution and allowable income levels change very often, be sure to check with your tax professional or brokerage firm for the most current IRS figures.

Eligibility   Unlike the traditional IRA, there is no 70 1/2 age limit on making contributions. The individual simply needs to have earned income equal to the amount contributed up to a maximum of $4,000 ($8,000 combined for spouses) per year.

Converting To Roth IRA   Traditional IRAs can be converted to a Roth IRA. However, there are some qualifications that must be met, and investors should carefully assess, with a qualified advisor, whether the conversion would be beneficial.

Keogh Plans

Self Employed Income   Anyone with self-employed income qualifies to enroll in a "Keogh" plan. They are specifically for self-employed persons. Usually doctors, lawyers, and other self employed professionals are chiefly among the Keogh participants.

Contributions   Keogh participants are allowed to contribute 25 % of income or $44,000, whichever is less.

Eligible Employees Any employee who is working full time (over 1000 hours per year) and has completed at least one years of service, must be included in the Keogh plan at the same rate as the employer. Only the first $150,000 of employer income is used to compute the average.

Withdrawals The rules for Keogh withdrawals are the same as those for IRAs. Withdrawals cannot begin without penalty before the age of 59 1/2. Similarly, withdrawals must begin by April 1 after the year the participant turns 70 1/2.

Penalties The penalties for early withdrawal are the same as as for IRAs. The withdrawal is taxed at the participants current tax rate, plus a "penalty" of 10%.

All IRA investments are permitted with one notable addition. Keogh plans allow cash value life insurance plans to be considered as an investment; IRAs do not.

Permitted Investments Once again please remember to check with a qualified tax consultant for the lastest updates on what investments may or may not be permitted. Congress changes retirement tax law very frequently.

Employer Based Plans

As you might expect, there are many more types of "employer" based plans than "individual" based plans. These plans can be very complex and might require the assistance of financial planners and tax attorneys. It is beyond the scope of this text to attempt to define or explain in detail the interworkings of these plans. But rather, my goal is to outline the basic plans that do exist and the primary characteristics of each.

Pension Plans

Defined Contribution Plan

As the name implies, contributions to these types of plans are predetermined or "defined" based on a formula set forth in the plan. This formula could be a specific percentage of profits or employee earnings. Irrespective of which factor is used, the contribution limits are the same: 25% of income, up to $44,000 per year.

Money Purchase Plan

Money purchase plans are based on a **percent of salary** contribution. The amount of the contribution must be deposited annually. Naturally, the longer an individual is with the company, the higher the salary. As the salary increases, so does the dollar amount of the contribution, therefore, this type of plan benefits the long-term employee much more than the short-term employee.

Defined Benefit

This type of plan seeks to provide a certain "benefit" to the plan participant at retirement. The contributions are determined by using actuarial tables. The longer one has to retirement, the lower the contribution; the shorter the term to retirement, the greater the contribution. Remember, this plan seeks to provide a fixed "dollar amount" at retirement, irrespective of the individuals age. This plan is much more beneficial to, relatively speaking, an older employee.

Unfunded Pension Liability

In a perfect world, this category would not exist. A corporation is not required to fund 100% of its pension requirement on an annual basis. It must only meet minimum percentages set forth by law. Obviously, this "unfunded" portion (money due employees) of pension benefits should be of the utmost concern for employees.

Non-Pension Retirement Plans

Profit Sharing Plan

Again as the name suggest, profit-sharing plans allow the corporation to share its profits with its employees. Actual contributions, while based on company profits, are typically determined by the **"plan trustee"**. Contributions made by the employer are tax deductible; some plans also allow for contributions by the employee which are also deductible. The maximum contribution for the profit-sharing plan is 15% of employee compensation up to $30,000. The account grows tax deferred.

Deferred Compensation Plan

Under this type of plan, a portion of the employee's compensation is "deferred" until retirement or death. A contract is drawn between employee and employer specifying the deferred amounts and the requirements for receiving the deferred payment. If the requirements are not met, **no** payment is made. This plan is "non-qualified" and requires no IRS approval, nor is it subject to federal legislation governing retirement plans.

Taxed-Deferred Annuities (TDA) 403b Plan

All plans listed previously, cover "for profit" entities. However, there are many employees in the U.S who are employed by **"non-profit"** organizations. Recognizing the need for retirement plan options for these employees, Congress enacted legislation giving certain annuities and mutual funds, structured in a particular way, tax deferred status. These plans are referred to as **"403b"** plans. They are today very widespread and are used by schools, hospitals, and most non-profit foundations.

The contributions are tax deductible, and the earning grow tax deferred. Generally, the maximum contribution for 403b plans is 25% of income, up to $15,000 per year. (as of 2006, very similar to the 401k program)

Payroll Deduction (401k) Plan

Under this type of plan, which is offered by most "**for-profit**" corporations, the employee is allowed to make contributions of a specified percent of compensation. The contributions are limited to 15% of compensation up to $15,000 per year (as of 2006). These contribution limits are periodically adjusted for inflation. As of this writing, $15,000 is the yearly maximum contribution.

Also, these plans offer the employee the additional advantage of having the employer "match" a portion of, or all of the employee's contribution. Most employers have guidelines stating what percentage of the employee's contribution they will match and the time parameters, if any, for the vesting period. Make no mistake, any "matching" by the employer is FREE MONEY. Any employee employed by a firm with a matching 401k plan must find a way to participate and should try to participate to the maximum allowable extent.

Another benefit of the 401k plan, is the provision which allows employees to "**borrow**" their own money for any purpose, including home ownership. When the loan option is utilized, the plan administrator will set up a repayment schedule using payroll deductions to service the loan. The loan must be repaid within certain parameters specified by the IRS. Always check with your admistrator for specific details of this option.

Of all retirement plans available to the average employee, the 401k, in my opinion, is the most beneficial. I want to impress upon you the most important point on the subject of employer match,.. this is FREE MONEY and should be utilized fully.

Solo 401k Plan

The solo 401K plan is relatively new being introduced in 2005. This plan provides many of the same benefits of "normal" 401K plans, with the very big exception is that is was designed by Congress for small business owners that only employed themselves or their spouses.

The primary benefit of the Solo 401K, is that it allows a self employed person to tax defer more savings than does the traditional options for the self employed, namely the SEP-IRA and the Somple IRA, both of which are discussed later in this chapter. The savings calculations of course change from time to time, always check with your tax professional for the most current analysis.

Roth 401K

Finally on 401K's, the lastest wrinkle from Congress is the "Roth 401K" introduced in the 2006, was supposed to expire in 2010 but was recently made permenant. Simply stated, this feature allows 401K employees to enoy the same benefits as those who invest in Roth IRA's. The employee designates what percentage of their contribution is to be considered a "Roth" 401K contribution. The big difference here is that the portion designated as a "Roth" contribution is not tax deductible, but also is not subject to any taxes when removed from the Roth 401k account afer the age of 59 1/2 of course.

This latest savings option seems to be one of the best offered thus far for the majority of workers, however, as stated before, always check with you tax or financial professional for the lastest analysis before making any financial desicions.

SEP IRA

Simplified Employee Pension (SEP): This plan was enacted to allow employers to provide retirement benefits to employees while limiting the paperwork and fiduciary responsibility usually associated with qualified retirement plans. Under this plan, the employer makes a contribution to an IRA set up by the employee and receives a deduction for the contribution.

Contributions made by the employer cannot exceed 15% of the employee's income, up to a maximum of $44,000 annually. The employer is required to contribute equal percentages to each employee's account. (This is a major reason for why SEP IRAs seem under utilized)

In addition, the employee is permitted to make a regular contribution ($4,000 for individual) to the account; the deductibility of which is determined according to the employee's adjusted gross income level.

SIMPLE   Savings Incentive Match Plan for Employees is primarily for small businesses. It was designed for ease of use for small enterprises with less than 100 employees who earn more than $5,000.00 per year.

The contribution limit is $10,000.00 per year with a $2,500 "catch-up" provision.

Summary Comments   As it becomes more and more apparent that social security will not be sufficient to provide for the retirement of the American worker, the U.S. Congress has attempted to provide the individual and the business community with numerous additional retirement planning options.

As we move into the future, there will, undoubtedly be more options made available to the employer and employee. The most important point to take away from this discussion is that YOU are responsible for your own financial retirement security. You should explore all options available and ask your employer for clarification on any issues which are unclear or ambiguous. Remember, it's your money, and your FUTURE.

11

Self Regulatory Organizations

"...Keep away from people who
try to belittle your ambitions.
Small people always do that,
but the really great make you
feel that you, too, can become
great..."

Mark Twain
(1835-1910)
American Author

SELF REGULATORY ORGANIZATIONS (SROs)

Self Regulatory Organizations are organizations in the securities industry developed primarily to promote, regulate, and adjudicate the securities industry. Probably the best expanded definition of these three
objectives, can be found in the Certificate of Incorporation of the
National Association of Securities Dealers. They are listed below:

Promote   To promote cooperative efforts in the investment banking and securities business, to standardize its principles
and practices, to promote high standards of commercial
honor, to encourage and promote among members obser-
vance of Federal and State securities law;

Regulate   To adopt, administer, and enforce rules of fair practice
and rules to prevent fraudulent and manipulative prac-
tices, and, in general, to promote just and equitable principles of trade for the protection of investors;

Adjudicate   To promote self-discipline among members, and to
investigate and adjudicate grievances between the public
and members, and between members.

Self-regulatory organizations are "**trade associations**" comprised of
dues paying members. These members, are afforded certain business
privileges, including the right to conduct business in a specific market,
and are generally charged with the responsibility of promoting its particular marketplace. For example, if a company wishes to act as a
over-the-counter market maker, it must first become a member of the
National Association of Securities Dealers (NASD). The NASD is not
the only, but surely the primary source of NASD marketplace promo-
tion. The NASD would perform all the functions listed above, as
would all other self-regulatory organizations.

There are many Self-Regulatory Organizations (SROs) in the securities industry. Some of the more well known SROs are listed below.

* New York Stock Exchange
* American Stock Exchange
* National Association of Securities Dealers
* Midwest Stock Exchange
* Philadelphia Stock Exchange
* Chicago Board of Options Exchange
* Municipal Securities Rulemaking Board

Securities and Exchange Commission

The Securities and Exchange Commission is not an SRO. The SEC is the official federal agency empowered by the U.S. Congress to enforce securities laws. The SEC encourages the SROs to promote the securities' laws enacted by the U.S. Congress.

The SEC encourages the SROs to live up to a "higher" standard of legal compliance. It requests that the SROs adhere to not only the "**letter**" of the law, but also the "**spirit**" of the law.

There are several distinctions between SROs and the SEC. However, the most important distinguishing factor: SROs are only civil in their punishment, meaning they can fine, censure, suspend, or expel individuals or members for rules' violations. The SEC is empowered to pursue civil or criminal procedures against individuals or organizations. Put more bluntly, the SEC can put people in **jail**, while SROs cannot.

SRO Summary

Self Regulatory Organizations serve individuals and member organizations in various ways. Chief among them is the avenue they provide to the individual investor for timely, fair, and affordable conflict resolution. As a whole, SROs are among the most positive and beneficial elements in the securities industry.

Epilogue

Congratulations!!!   You've just completed the first step in securing your family's financial future. However, the learning process must not end here. As stated previously, the financial marketplace is dynamic, forever evolving and becoming more complicated. If you intend to prudently invest, to achieve the goals and objectives most of us share, such as the ability to pay for college tuition, provide for a stable and secure retirement, as well as to add more disposable income to your current lifestyle, then continuing to review this material as well as other related information is vital.

You must also understand, there is no substitute for "actual" experience. In other words, you must get in the game to realistically learn and understand the game. Let me draw an analogy. If one should desire to learn to play golf, it would be advisable to gather relevant literature on the subject, read and study this literature, and even engage in question and answer sessions with experienced golfers. The aspiring golf player could read and talk as much and as often as possible, BUT,..he or she will NOT learn how to swing the golf club UNTIL they actually pick up a golf club and start to practice. This is also true of investing. While it is advisable to learn as much as possible first, and seek out the advice and counsel of experienced investors, you will not fully comprehend the nuances of investing until you actually INVEST. This is not to suggest that you should take all of your retirement nest egg or savings and "throw" it in the stockmarket. You should, however, take a small portion, and BUY something. Even if it is only 1 share of a particular company in which you have an interest. The process of opening a brokerage account, depositing the funds, placing the order, and receiving the confirmation of purchase, will give you more familiarity with the process and this newfound familiarity will provide newfound comfort and confidence. Just remember, even the most seasoned professional was at some point a novice, placing his/her first trade. Sooner or later you must pick up the golf club and take a swing in order to learn golfing. The same is true with investing.

I sincerely believe that if you read these pages carefully you now possess the knowledge and skills necessary to take control of your own financial future. Now the question is what will you do with this knowledge? Investing has many perils which should not be overlooked. However, investment education coupled with courage, and patience will prove to be a great benefit in attaining financial security for you and your family. Do well, and you can do more good.

I hear and I forget.
I see and I remember.
I do and I understand.
Confucius (551-479 B.C.) Chinese philosopher

Glossary

Accrued Interest Interest which accumulates between interest payments on certain bonds. When a bond is purchased, this interest must added to the purchase price and remitted to the seller.

American Depository Receipt (ADR) An equity security, which trades on U.S. stock exchanges representing an ownership interest in foreign securities.

American Stock Exchange A financial market place which trades primarily shares of smaller companies and derivatives.

Assets The value of property owned.

Authorized Stock The number of shares which may be issued according to a corporations charter.

Balance Sheet The document prepared by businesses which accounts for all assets, liabilities, and equity of the business.

Beneficial Owner The actual owner of securities held in street name.

Bond A long term debt security which pays interest to its owner.

Book Entry A security which does not exist in paper form, but rather as a computer entry only.

Breakout When the price of a particular security suddenly rises above its average high price.

Breakpoint Point where sales charge discounts may apply.

Budget Deficit   Planned (realized) expenses are greater than planned (realized) revenues.

Budget Surplus   Planned (realized) revenues are greater than planned (realized) expenses.

Buying Power   The amount of money available to investors for securities purchases through the borrowing of money from a stockbrokerage firm.

Central Bank   The governmental institution given the responsibility of regulating the money supply and interest rates.

Certificates of Deposits   A short term debt security, with low risk which comparatively yields a low rate of interest.

Chart   A graphical depiction of numerical data. Generally used to depict price, and volume, over a particular time continuum.

Closed End Fund   A type of mutual fund, which does not issue new shares on a continuous basis. The fund makes a one time issuance of shares, and then becomes "closed". These shares trade on stock exchanges in the same manner as common stock.

Commercial Paper   A short term debt security, usually used for corporate financing of less than 270 days.

Consumer Price Index   A leading economic indicator, which measures the prices of a basket of consumer goods and used as an indicator of future price direction.

Currency   A country's paper money. Currencies are also traded as securities in financial markets.

Dealer   An individual or firm which purchases securities from the general public for its own inventory.

Debenture   Intermediate and long debt security issued by corporations backed only by the full faith and credit of the issuer. Their is no collateral backing the debt issue.

Debt Security   Any security which does not represent and ownership interest in a company. Usually requires the issuing entity to repay principal plus a predetermined rate of interest.

Deflation   The occurrence of decreasing prices and/or values of assets. The opposite of inflation.

Depression   A sustained low level of economic output usually combined with a relatively high level of unemployment.

Derivatives   A security created and based upon some other underlying security. Options are an example of derivatives.

Discount   The amount a security is priced below its fair or par value.

Discount Broker   A stockbrokerage firm which typically does not give investment advice, and usually charges lower commissions.

Discount Rate   The interest rate at which money is loaned from the Federal Reserve to member banks. Many consumer loans are tied to the discount rate, making it one of the most effective monetary policy tools of the Federal Reserve.

Dividend The portion of net profits which are distributed to shareholders. Usually distributed on a quarterly basis.

Earning Per Share Net profits divided by the number of shares outstanding. A key fundamental analysis figure.

Economics Study of societal output of good and services.

Equity The portion of asset value which remains after all debts and obligations have been met.

Equity security Any security which represents an ownership interest or a right for ownership interest in a company.

Eurodollars U.S. dollar denominated deposits in foreign banks.

ETF's Hybrid mutual funds covering various industries.

Federal Call The amount of money required to be deposited when making a purchase through a margin account.

Federal Funds Moneys that are on deposit at the Federal Reserve Bank and are available to be loaned to other banks.

Federal Reserve The central bank of the United States. Responsible for monetary policy including the setting of interest rates.

Financial Statements Documents which state the financial condition of a particular company. Examples: Balance Sheet and Income Statement.

Firm Bid
A quote to either buy or sell a security which will be honored for a particular time period. Generally used with the trading of fixed income securities.

First Market
Any shares traded on a "Listed" exchange, (ie. NYSE, AMEX, etc.) are considered to be traded in the "First Market".

Fiscal Policy
Policy which is developed and implemented through the federal government. (Legislative policy)

Floor Trader
A stockbroker who works on the actual stock exchange floor. Floor brokers generally assist in the execution of their firms customer orders.

Fourth Market
Consists of institutional investors who trade directly with one another.

Fund Family
Mutual funds which are all offered by the same company. For example: Scudder funds, Fidelity Funds.

Fund Sponsor
The company which brings the mutual fund public.

Fundamental Analysis
Type of security analysis which primarily analyzes companies and attempts to answer the question of in "which" company to invest.

Gross Domestic Product
The measure of economic output for the overall economy.

Growth Fund
A mutual fund which invest in "high growth" stocks.

Hedge Fund   A fund which generally consist of only "accredited" investors. These funds participate in riskier strategies and securities.

Hypothecation   The practice of pledging customers securities as collateral for a brokerage firm loan.

Income Fund   A mutual fund which seeks to generate investment income for its participants.

Indenture   The portion of a bond issue which list all the specific requirements and terms of the issue.

Individual Retirement Account (IRA)   An investment account which is granted special tax deferred treatment from the U.S. Government given certain stipulations and conditions.

Inflation   The economic occurrence of higher and higher prices. Generally caused by an overheated economy and an oversupply of money in the economy.

Initial Public Offering   The act of offering shares to the public for the first time. Also referred to as an IPO.

Intrinsic Value   The portion of an options price which represents the in-the-money value.

Investment Advisor   An individual or firm which assist in the development and implementation of a financial or investment plan.

Issued Stock   Stock which is currently in the market place. Usually only a portion of "authorized stock".

Junk Bond	A high yielding fixed income security. Usually issued by corporations.
Keogh Account	A retirement account granted special tax deferred treatment by the U.S. Government. This account is generally used by self employed professionals such as doctors, lawyers, etc.
Keynesian Theory	An economic theory which advocates, as its premise, that governments should utilize borrowing and spending in an attempt to spur economic growth and full employment.
Liabilities	The value of obligations owed to others.
Long	The term used to denote that the investor is an owner of securities and is therefore expecting market appreciation.
Maintenance Call	A request for an additional money deposit to a margin account generally caused by a drop in the value of the securities held in the account.
Margin	The borrowing of money from a brokerage firm.
Market Maker	An individual or firm who acts as a middle man between investors who are buying and selling securities. This term generally applies to "middle men" participating in the NASD and OTC market.
Market Order	Instructs your stockbroker to execute your buy or sell order at the current trading price.
Market Value	The value of securities as measured at current prices.

Monetary Policy Policy developed and implemented by the Federal Reserve. Involves the setting of interest rates, and the supply of money.

Money Market Debt securities, short term, usually purchased in amounts of $1.00 per share.

Moving Average A technical analysis tool used in an attempt to "smooth" out market price fluctuations. Is derived by summing a group of price points, then dividing the outcome by the number of price points in the group.

Municipal Bonds Long term debt securities issued by local governments. Are also granted favorable tax treatment by Congress.

Mutual Fund A group of money pooled by investors which is professionally managed, diversified, and adheres to a particular investment objective. Can be either "closed end" or "open end".

NASD The regulatory body which licenses all stockbrokers and regulates the OTC stock market.

Net Asset Value The value or price of mutual funds. This value is per share and generally calculated once a day using closing prices.

Net Worth The value remaining after all debts, liabilities, and obligations have been satisfied.

New York Stock Exchange The preeminent marketplace for the trading of equity securities. Utilizes an "auction" trading environment.

No Load Fund	A mutual fund which does not charge a fee or "load" to purchase its shares.
Open End Fund	A mutual fund which does not have a limit on the number of shares which it can issue. The fund has an unlimited or "open" share authorization.
Outstanding Shares	The number of a shares issued and currently held by the general public. Shares owned by the corporation are not included in this figure.
Preferred Stock	An equity security whose owners have a "preference" over common stockholders as to the payment of dividends, and in the case of dissolution, the distribution of assets.
Premium	The portion of a securities price which is over and above its fair or par market value.
Primary Dealer	A firm which is granted a "special" privilege of dealing directly with the Federal Reserve for the purpose of purchasing and reselling treasury securities.
Primary Market	The market where "new issues" are sold to the public. Shares are not traded in this market, they are initially sold, then held until the issue begins "publicly" trading.
Prospectus	The document distributed by all mutual funds which outlines in detail all the specifics of that particular fund.
Proxy	A document used to vote on shareholder issues in absentia. It also grants authority for others to vote for the proxy holder.

Recession　　　　Occurs when economic output declines. Technically, an economic decline for two consecutive quarters.

Redemption Fee　　A fee charged by mutual funds, assessed on shareholders who sell their shares before a pre-specified time period.

Refunding　　　　The process of selling new securities, usually debt securities, to repay, or retire previously issued debt.

Registrar　　　　Usually a bank, which has the responsibility of keeping the names and addresses of stockholders and ensuring that the corporation does not issue more shares than allowed by its charter.

Resistance　　　　The price level at which a security seems to be unable to rise above.

Rights　　　　　An offer to current shareholders which allows the purchase of securities at a below market price, and allows shareholders to retain their current proportional ownership position.

Risk　　　　　A dangerous element or hazard causing the possibility of loss or injury.

Second Market　　The Over-the-Counter (OTC) market. Securities trading **not** conducted on any listed Exchange.

Secondary Market　The marketplace where "existing" securities are traded. This market does **not** include any IPO placements.

Self Regulatory Organization	An industry association developed to promote, regulate, and adjudicate its particular association.
Selling Short	The borrowing of securities from a brokerage firm to sell to other investors. This is a bearish strategy.
Settlement	The day when a securities trade becomes complete. Currently 3 business days for stock transactions.
Sinking Fund	A fund into which money is deposited on a regular basis for the expressed purpose of retiring a particular debt issue.
Specialized Fund	A type of mutual fund which specializes in a particular industry or geographic region. For example a "gold fund" or "international fund" would be classified as "specialized" funds.
Stock	An equity security which represents an ownership interest in a particular company.
Stock Exchange	A marketplace which exist for the purpose of facilitating securities transactions.
Stock Split	When the number of shares are increased and the currently market value is decreased proportionately. Also called a stock dividend.
Street Name	Shares held at brokerage firms are registered in the name of the brokerage firm. Shares held under this registration are said to be held in "street name".
Subordinated Debenture	Debt issues which hold a lower status of security in the event of dissolution.
Technical	The type of securities analysis which attempts

Analysis   to answer the question of "when" to purchase.

Third Market   Trading of "listed" securities which takes place off the floor of an exchange.

Trade Deficit   When the dollar value of imports exceeds that of exports.

Trade Surplus   When the dollar value of exports exceed that of imports.

Transfer Agent   Usually a bank, it has the responsibility of maintaining securities transaction records, disseminating corporate information to shareholders, and issuing new shares to purchasers while canceling existing shares of sellers.

Treasury Stock   Stock which is repurchased by corporations and held inventory.

Trust Indenture   A document which details all the specifics of a particular debt issue, but which is required to be monitored by an independently appointed trust bank.

Unsystematic Risk   Risks which are specific to a particular issuer or company rather than to the market as a whole.

Yield   The return on a particular investment.

Zero Coupon   Fixed income security which pays no interest, ("0") to the owner, but rather adds the interest to the principal and accumulates during the term of the security.

Index

www.ingramcontent.com/pod-product-compliance
Lightning Source LLC
Chambersburg PA
CBHW080526220326
41599CB00032B/6211